trotman

Media

UNCOVERED

*Other titles in the Careers Uncovered series
published by Trotman*

trotman

CATHERINE HARRIS

Media

UNCOVERED

Media Uncovered
This first edition published in 2004 by Trotman and Company Ltd
2 The Green, Richmond, Surrey TW9 1PL

Publishing salaries reproduced with kind permission from
bookcareers.com, © bookcareers.com, Salary Survey 2002.

Editorial and Publishing Team

Author Catherine Harris
Editorial Mina Patria, Editorial Director; Rachel Lockhart,
Commissioning Editor; Anya Wilson, Editor; Bianca Knights,
Assistant Editor
Production Ken Ruskin, Head of Pre-press and Production
Sales and Marketing Deborah Jones, Head of Sales and Marketing
Advertising Tom Lee, Commercial Director
Managing Director Toby Trotman

Designed by **XAB**

British Library Cataloguing in Publication Data
A catalogue record for this book is available
from the British Library

ISBN 1 84455 000 1

Typeset by ... Book ... Limited,

Printed and ... in Great ... Press,
... Trowbridge, Wiltshire

CONTENTS

About the Author

Catherine Harris is a freelance journalist. She has written for national newspapers including the *Guardian*, the *Evening Standard* and the *Sunday Mirror*. She has also worked as a researcher in TV and radio at the BBC and in independent production companies. *Media Uncovered* is her third book.

Acknowledgements

Researching this book was great fun as I met so many wonderful people. Thanks so much to all those who agreed to be interviewed about their glorious media careers. Thanks also to everyone at Trotman for all their help.

CHAPTER 1

Why read this book?

This book offers an overview of working in the media. It will give you an idea of what media jobs entail so you can start thinking about whether a job in the media is for you. We've given you lots of leads to follow up. This book is a fantastic place to start research into your future. If you find the right industry and the right job for you, the reward will be a fulfilling, satisfying and enjoyable career. Who knows, you might actually look forward to the alarm going off in the morning!

This book is packed with real-life case studies. We've gone undercover and spoken to people working in loads of different media jobs in the UK. They've told us the truth – warts and all – about what it's like to do their job. They also offer advice about how to get in and get on in their area.

The media is a broad term covering a range of different sectors, different jobs and different products. But there is one thing that all jobs in the media have in common: they are highly competitive. To get in and get on you have to have talent, determination and the ability to make the most of every situation. Each one of our case studies says successful media careers are made on long hours. But most say it's worth it, because they love the job.

It is difficult to get into the media. If, having done your research, you still want to work in the media – go for it. During the research for this book I spoke to a successful BBC TV news reporter. She told me that after university she applied to one of the most prestigious MA courses in the country for broadcast journalism. Not only did she not get a place, her interviewers told her she should think of a different career – they didn't think she'd make it as a journalist. If she'd listened to them she would have given up before she'd started. Instead, she applied for a different course, secured a place and went from strength to strength, eventually landing a plum job in broadcasting. What's the moral of the story? Don't be put off too easily. Hard work and focus can help you overcome obstacles and achieve your goals. Always listen to advice, but the only person who can decide whether you would suit a particular career is you.

CHAPTER 2

Working in the media

A CHANGING MEDIA LANDSCAPE

It's an exciting time to start a career in the media. Innovations like wireless technology and broadband are changing the media environment. From book publishing to radio and newspapers, all media sectors are embracing new technologies as a means of communicating and interacting with their viewers, readers and listeners.

The possibility of transmitting DVD-quality video over broadband is having a significant impact on the broadcasting landscape. The BBC has announced plans to offer some of its vast historic archives online with a view to total digital accessibility, so that viewers can pick and choose what to watch at any time.

And with Sony and Microsoft investing in online gaming – allowing players to compete over broadband networks – it's easy to see the massive impact of broadband on all media sectors.

Convergence is the buzz-word of the media's near future. One possibility is that TV, as we know it, will become a thing of the past.

The new home appliance will be a media centre, something between a TV and a PC. It will be able to play and store music, videos and photos and will have a built-in personal video recorder. In fact, Microsoft has already launched a product that does all these things.

The government is backing technological change in the media all the way. According to some, the digital revolution isn't coming – it's already here. A government target has been set to have 100 per cent digital TV usage in the UK by 2010. At the last count, in December 2003, just over half of UK households owned a digital TV, according to Ofcom. But some media commentators say the digital revolution is being over-hyped and that the government will have to reconsider the feasibility of a total digital switchover by 2010. The point is: the future of the media is being carved out now. No one knows for sure exactly what the future holds. You could be part of that future.

DOG EAT DOG

A huge number of people want to work in the media. Every year around 60,000[1] hopefuls try to break into the UK audio-visual industries (film, TV, radio and interactive media). There are only 200,000 people working in the audio-visual industries, so you can see that it's highly competitive. You can increase your chances by doing your research well and building up experience for a specific part of the media.

In general, the more creative a job is, the more sought-after it is. New entrants often overlook jobs in the business and finance sides of media sectors. This is a mistake. If you are numerate, have strong organisational skills and are good at detailed work, these positions offer increased stability, and sometimes offer greater longevity. Other job areas may be less secure. For example, production jobs in TV are dominated by a freelance youth workforce. The average age of people working in TV production is 39, and the majority are aged between 25 and 30[2]. Apart from being a good route into the media, a financial media background can be useful in attaining a senior management position. This is true in publishing and new media too.

[1] *Skills for Tomorrow's Media*, Skillset, 2001
[2] Skillset Freelance Survey 2001

If you're starting out in media you should look at the opportunities presented by the changing technological media environment. In times of rapid change, becoming an expert in a new area can give you a career advantage. Practical skills relating to new technologies will stand you in good stead to capitalise on opportunities offered by the changing environment. At the time of publication, the BBC was advertising for exceptional people with a specific interest in editorial, design or technical areas to help shape the future of BBC Interactive.

FREELANCE OR FULL TIME

Once you do get in you can work either as a freelance – being your own boss and moving from contract to contract – or as a staffer – working full time for a single organisation. Freelance work can leave you financially high and dry: there's no holiday pay, and when your contract finishes you have to find new work, fast. However, rates are generally good because of the insecurity, and freelance work does allow people more flexibility. In theory freelancers should be able to take months off when they need to, rather than being fixed to holiday terms decided by an organisation. Read the case studies in this book – from a mixture of freelancers and staffers – and decide which you would prefer.

AREAS OF THE MEDIA

In this book we've divided the media up into the following areas:

- TV

- Film

- Radio

- Newspapers and magazines

- Books and publishing

- New media.

The possibilities for a new career are endless, with each area offering far-reaching opportunities. You may dream of being a presenter on Radio 4 or a DJ on a music station. Or you may want to work in academic publishing as opposed to children's or blockbuster romantic fiction. Whatever your interests, you can pursue them in a media career.

As each area is discussed in more detail later on, you will see there are opportunities for crossover. A standard career path for a broadcast news journalist, for example, often encompasses both radio and TV reporting; and local newspaper reporting is a good route into online news writing.

New technologies in broadcasting are likely to shift the traditional definitions in the media sector even further. Being flexible and adaptable has always been part of working in the media. Read up as much as you can about the wider media context. Understanding the changing relationships in the converging media landscape could help you on your way to an exciting and varied career.

WHO THE BIGWIGS ARE - TOP JOBS IN MEDIA

According to the *Guardian*, these are considered the top jobs in media:

- Director General, BBC – Mark Thompson*

- Chairman and Chief Executive, News Corporation – Rupert Murdoch

- Chairman, Ofcom – David Currie

- Chairman, BBC – Michael Grade*

- Chairman, British Telecom – Sir Christopher Bland

- Editor, the *Sun* – Rebekah Wade

- Editor-in-Chief, Associated Newspapers – Paul Dacre

- Chief Executive, Ofcom – Stephen Carter

- Chief Executive, Northern and Shell, Express Newspapers – Richard Desmond

- Competition Commissioner, European Union – Mario Monti.

Source: *Media Guardian 2003*

* Mark Thompson and Michael Grade are recent appointments following the resignations of senior BBC figures after the Hutton Inquiry in 2004.

All these people have excelled in the media environment and come out on top. To find out more information, like how much they earn and what age they are, go to the fantastic media guardian website, www.guardian.co.uk – the mother of all media websites!

Everybody on our bigwigs list once started with the simple idea that working in the media might be for them. For some inspiration, do some research into their careers and find out how they got to where they are today. You never know, in a few years' time, it could be you.

WINNERS OF THE ETHNIC MULTICULTURAL MEDIA AWARDS (EMMA)

People from ethnic minorities are under-represented in the media. BECTU, the largest broadcasting union, has called TV 'institutionally racist', and Greg Dyke, the former BBC Director General, once described the BBC as 'hideously white'. Only 8.2 per cent of the workforce in the audio-visual industries is from ethnic minorities. However, the number of ethnic minority media employees is rising. The Ethnic Multicultural Media Awards celebrate diversity and professional excellence in the media industry. Awards are also given to key media figures who are perceived to be committed to cross-cultural communications and anti-racist attitudes. David Beckham was deemed eligible for an award from the EMMA foundation as a sportsman who 'crosses all multicultural boundaries' and 'represents a positive message'. For more information about EMMA and the awards go to www.emma.uk.com.

SOME EMMA AWARDS 2004

- Best Film Production – *The Passion of The Christ*

- Best Film Actor – Tom Cruise (*The Last Samurai*)

- Best Film Actress – Maia Morgenstern (*The Passion of The Christ*)

- Best TV Production – *Teachers*

- Best TV Actor – Art Malik (*Holby City*)

- Best TV Actress – Parminder Nagra (*Second Generation*)

- Best Book/Novel – *The Bookseller of Kabul*

- Best Comedy/Comedian – Inder Manocha

- Best Print Journalist – Yasmin Alibhai-Brown

- Best Radio News Journalist – Vanessa Feltz

- Best News Journalist – Lisa Aziz

- Best TV Documentary – *The Secret Policeman*

- Media Personality of the Year – Greg Dyke

- Sporting Personalities of the Year – David Beckham and Thierry Henry

- Legend Award – Bruce Lee.

Source: www.emma.uk.com

These people were chosen because they have achieved excellence in their media field. Find out more about their careers and listen to or watch their output. Take some tips from the top and learn from those who are really good at what they do. You could be one of the next generation to make it big in the media. One day it could be you winning an EMMA award.

CHAPTER 3

Jobs in tv

TV QUIZ

Here's a quick quiz to give you an idea of some of the skills needed to work in TV.

1) You're a runner in an independent production company. You've worked a nine-hour day and are on your way home, but the development producer asks you to look through some casting tapes for a new presenter for a programme aimed at 16–24-year-olds – she thinks that you will be able to give a youth angle.

   a) You're tired so you tell the producer you are going home but are happy to look at them tomorrow.
   b) You say you can't help as you don't know anything about casting.
   c) You'd love to help as you watch a lot of TV and have got loads of ideas about what makes a good presenter.

2) You're a researcher on a three-part documentary about dating. Shooting starts tomorrow. It's 6pm and one of the couples you've confirmed has had an argument and no longer

wants to take part in the programme. You've got to find a replacement and fast.

a) You work with the team and call everyone you know to try and find a new couple. When that doesn't work, you go out on the street and ask random people. Eventually you persuade the best friend of the couple who dropped out to take part, but not until midnight that night!
b) You collapse under the stress, start crying and go out and get drunk.
c) You leave it up to the assistant producer – after all, he gets paid more money.

3) You've been promoted from a runner to a position buying transmission rights for the music and archive footage on a current production. You are in charge of the budget and have to convert dollars to pounds sterling. You have to stay late most nights to deal with companies in Los Angeles.

a) You leave at 6.30pm on the dot. They can't expect you to stay any later on what they're paying you.
b) Figures have never been your strong point and you mess up, overspending massively on the budget.
c) You work efficiently. You stay late, but not every night, and your budget comes in bang on target.

ANSWERS:

1) The correct answer is (c). You're a runner, so it will be expected that you are dying to get on. It may be late, but the producer is asking you to help and giving you an opportunity to learn. Runners who get promoted not only demonstrate that they can work hard, they must also show they are genuinely interested in the industry.

2) The correct answer is (a). Working in TV, you will constantly be in situations in which you have to troubleshoot, and quickly. Lots of things can go wrong so everyone on the team has to be able to come up with quick solutions to problems.

3) The correct answer is (c). Being able to handle a budget is an important part of many jobs in production. The flexibility to stay late is also an important part of working on productions.

TV OVERVIEW

Of all media careers, jobs in TV are probably the most sought after – look at these numbers.

FASCINATING FACTS

60,000: the number of people who try to work in TV, radio and film – of those 60,000 a large proportion want to work in TV.
60,000: the number of people already working in TV in 2002.
38,500: people working in broadcast and independent TV companies.

IT'S A RATINGS GAME

Ratings are hugely important in TV. While the BBC can afford to be slightly less ratings-driven than commercial channels, most TV shows are required to get a big audience fast or they are likely to be dumped or shelved to a less popular time slot. Imagine that happening to something you'd sweated blood and guts over. Ratings are measured by the Broadcasters' Audience Research Board (BARB), an organisation that knows the viewing habits of 10,000 people in 5,100 homes.

Worldwide spin-offs are also becoming increasingly important. The British are the second largest TV exporters in the world. With formats like *Pop Idol* and *Survivor* selling around the world, British shows make up around 13 per cent of the global TV exports market. But that's nothing compared to American TV exports, which account for 68 per cent of global TV imports. Long-running sensations like *Sex and the City* and *Friends* have finally come to an end – but their global success has been phenomenal. The final episode of *Friends* was an international news story.

In 2002 the UK made £666 million in export television sales. The Americans spent £232 million on British TV programmes.

Source: British Television Distributors
Association/DCMS 2002

TV'S BIGGEST EMPLOYERS

- The **BBC** – employs over 26,000 people, including around 14,500 in-house programme makers.

- **Channel 4** and **five tv** – both channels commission content from independent production companies rather than employing in-house programme makers. Around 900 people work for Channel 4 in other roles, such as commissioning and publicity, while around 250 people work directly for five tv.

- **Carlton** – employs 2,800 people and owns broadcasters across the UK providing output for ITV.

- **Granada** – employs 5,000 people and owns broadcasters across the UK providing output for ITV.

- **ITN** – employs around 750 people, mainly providing news for Channel 4, five tv and independent radio.

- **Independent production companies (indies)** – There are around 1,000 independent production companies across the UK.

TOP TIP

Have a look at www.bbc.co.uk/jobs/ for a fantastic overview of the opportunities available if you work for the UK's public service broadcaster.
Go to www.ideasfactory.com for an impressive careers site with information and ideas on everything from TV to new media.

REAL LIVES – THE FREELANCE LIVE DIRECTOR/PRODUCER ON KIDS' TV

Graham Gordon, 28, London

The job

My job is coming up with ideas to fill the airtime and working with an associate producer, director and a runner to make scintillating, captivating live TV. Things can go wrong when you're live and that's the buzz. Anything can happen. You can make the best TV or the worst TV. In theory if you rehearse well enough nothing should go wrong but that doesn't always happen in practice. When it goes well it's a fast and fun job. Live TV is like juggling on a motorbike!

Best bit

The buzz, putting an idea into practice and putting it out live, it's happening there and then so it's reactive and interactive. Usually there is a fun bunch of people working in kids' TV, everyone's up for a laugh. Most people working in live production are in their twenties and early thirties – except the technical people, who tend to be more a mix of ages. Live production is quite draining, so I think inevitably people move on after a bit. It's a young person's game in the sense that it's exhausting. A lot of people go into management in their forties.

Worst bit

Security in TV – there's very little when you're freelance. Most people worry about that. But the upside of job insecurity is that people give their all. So everyone is pushing themselves and doing the best they can. That makes for a very creative environment. The other downside of TV is there are some arrogant and pretentious people around. But you get used to that.

Career path

Once I'd got in as a runner it was just a question of making contacts and developing my skills. I didn't do any courses. I just learnt on the job and started picking up DIGITAL VIDEO skills as soon as possible – that's key to getting on. I took any work I could get but I always knew I wanted to direct and that's what I aimed for. I moved from company to company getting as much experience as possible on each job.

Career Ladder

Freelance Live Kids' TV director/producer
↑
Disney Channel producer/director
↑
Director for Paramount and Trouble
↑
Researcher, AP Independent production company specialising in kids' TV
↑
Researcher, Children's Channel
↑
Head Runner, at Nickelodeon
↑
Runner, facilities house in Soho
↑
Assistant, Thresher's wine merchants
↑
English at university

JARGON BUSTER

Runner, otherwise known as general dogsbody. Entry-level job in the industry: so-called because it entails so much running around!

JOBS IN TV

CREATORS AND PRODUCTION

This involves coming up with ideas for programmes, developing ideas, putting those ideas into practice and making them happen. From *Who Wants to be a Millionaire?* to *EastEnders*, TV shows are made through the blood, sweat and tears of a team of people turning a creative idea into TV reality. For most of these roles DIGITAL VIDEO (DV) skills are increasingly useful.

This area includes roles such as:

- **Producer** – puts a programme and team together. The job requires creativity and organisation and the ability to handle budgets. In some strands, such as documentaries, the producer may also be the director.

- **Director** – uses his or her creative vision to shape the look and often content of a programme. In charge of the set and filming. In drama, the director is the big cheese.

- **Scriptwriter** – writes scripts on existing soaps or dramas or comedies or creates an original script for a new programme or series.

- **Assistant producer** – works with the producer and director to generate ideas and make the programme happen. In documentaries, this role will often involve securing case studies and probably some filming.

- **Presenter** – the face of a programme. Needs to perform well consistently, often under pressure.

- **Researcher** – one rung down from the assistant producer. Has ideas, finds case studies if necessary and researches programme content. Can be helpful to know how to use a DV camera.

- **Production assistant** – an assistant to the production department, a mainly administrative role but a good place to learn from.

SKILLED TECHNICAL AND ARTISTIC PEOPLE

TV is a technical business. Nothing would happen without a skilled team of technical experts to facilitate the director and producer's vision and transmit the programme. Even better, there are some technical areas with skills gaps, where well-trained people are always needed. These include production accountants, broadcast and electrical engineers and carpenters.

Includes roles such as:

- **Floor manager/assistant director** – manages the studio from the floor. On location this role is called an assistant director.

- **Lighting camera operator** – sets up and operates the camera in studio and on location.

- **Camera supervisor** – co-ordinates a team of lighting camera operators.

- **Editor** – cuts footage together with the director/producer. An editor needs to be both highly technical, visual and a perfectionist.

- **Sound technician** – uses equipment such as a boom. Sound technicians are responsible for a programme's sound.

- **Broadcast engineer** – designs, maintains and operates broadcast equipment.

- **Production designer, art director, set designer** – are responsible for the design and creation of the set.

BUSINESS, LEGAL AND FINANCE

TV is a business. Someone's got to see the big picture and count the money! Without the business and finance people, the TV industry would collapse.

These areas include roles such as:

- **Rights assistant** – deals with contracts, release forms (legal forms signed by contributors to permit broadcasters to transmit their content) and other legal administration, including rights issues relating to archive footage.

- **Media law expert and contract expert** – all broadcasters and many larger independent production companies have their own in-house lawyers to deal with everything from presenter contracts to worldwide transmission rights.

- **Production accountant** – handles the budget on production, ensuring budget is not under- or overspent.

- **Press officer** – works for a broadcaster or an independent production company, publicises new shows and maintains the company's profile and reputation.

BROADCAST JOURNALISTS

They tell the news. This is a fast-paced job, and the quality of news stories rests on the team's ability to research, interview and communicate the news.

- **Editor** – responsible for the overall news programme, makes editorial decisions and decides the news agenda and structure of the programme.

- **Producer** – works on individual stories within a news programme, either with or without a correspondent, depending on the needs of the story.

- **Presenter** – presents news programmes, often live, including interviews. Experience and broadcast skills are a must.

- **Correspondent** – a specialist news reporter, an expert in his/her journalistic area, researches stories and broadcasts TV reports, sometimes live. Experience and broadcast skills essential.

CASH

Salaries in TV start pretty low, but they do increase as you climb the ladder. These figures give you an idea of what the average person gets paid for the following jobs. Huge variations do apply, especially at more senior level, where large remuneration is available.

PROGRAMME-MAKING AND JOURNALISM

Broadcast Assistant	£16,000–£25,000
Production Assistant	£15,000–£30,000
Researcher	£16,000–£35,000
Script Editor	£20,000–£25,000
Assistant Producer	£25,000–£35,000
Floor Manager	£25,000–£40,000
Reporter	£25,000–£45,000
Producer	£30,000–£50,000 plus
Series Producer	£35,500–£55,000 plus
Director	£32,000–£50,000 plus
Presenter	£35,000–£100,000 plus

TECHNICAL AND ARTISTIC JOBS

Wardrobe Mistress/Master	£500–£1,000 a week (freelance)
Make-up Artist	£500–£1,000 a week (freelance)
Art Director	£600–£1,300 a week (freelance)
Sound Technician	£15,000–£30,000 plus
Camera Operator	£500–£1,300 a week (freelance)
Broadcast Engineer	£22,000–£50,000 plus

BUSINESS JOBS

Personal Assistant	£18,000–£25,000
Schedules Assistant	£18,000–£25,000
Advertising Sales Executive	£20,000–£30,000
Press Officer	£25,000–£35,000
Brand Manager	£25,000–£40,000
Head of Acquisitions	£40,000–£60,000

Source: *Creative Careers: TV*, Milly Jenkins

TOP TIP

For more in-depth info on TV jobs and the industry, read *Creative Careers: TV* by Milly Jenkins, published by Trotman in association with Channel 4'S IDEASFACTORY.

REAL LIVES – THE NEWS CORRESPONDENT

A 33-year-old BBC TV correspondent, London

The job
My job combines a mixture of researching interesting stories, writing, going out and filming and talking to extraordinary people about what they've done. Being a TV news reporter is a sociable job. We work in teams. I film with a camera crew and work with an editor. I also like working under pressure. I enjoy the discipline of deadlines. The deadline forces you to write accurately, quickly and hopefully entertainingly in the time slot you are allocated to deliver the story.

Best bit
I'm constantly trying to improve my broadcast techniques and developing how I tell a story and how I use pictures. It never gets boring.

Worst bit
It's most difficult when there isn't a story there and you're asked by an editor to make a story out of nothing. The easiest pieces are strong stories. Often I will have to battle with an editor when I don't think the story is strong enough. However, if the editor thinks it's a story, you've got to do it and it can be a real struggle finding something to say.

Career path
After university I did a postgrad diploma in broadcast journalism at the London College of Printing and then I went into local radio in London – News Direct – and worked as a reporter. I spent a couple of years there and then I moved to IRN and worked as a reporter on national radio. After two years I made the move to TV reporting and reported on the ITV news channel. While I was there I did ITV breakfast news and lunchtime news. After about a year I went freelance and worked as a TV news reporter for ITN and BBC London. I then took a short-term contract at the BBC doing national news reports and subsequently was offered a staff position. Now I'm one of the BBC's specialist news correspondents.

Career Ladder

BBC staff TV news reporter
↑
Freelance TV news reporter
↑
News Reporter, independent national TV
↑
News Reporter, independent national radio
↑
News Reporter, independent local radio
↑
Broadcast Journalism MA
↑
French at university

JARGON BUSTER

Rushes – uncut film that needs to be edited so it can be shaped into the programme.

REAL LIVES – THE EX-TV RESEARCHER

Jenny Power, 34, photographer

I started off doing work experience at the BBC and worked in arts documentaries. That was wonderful and I loved it, the people were great and I thought I wanted to make TV my career. Then I got my first job in the independent sector in a well-known London production company that produced popular and light entertainment shows. I really hated it. I hated the culture, the fact that everybody name-dropped, the fact that they always tried to diddle me on my contract and the fact that they were paying me so little when I was working so hard. There was no one in there to support the juniors. The corporate attitude was pay the big producers and directors well and treat all the junior staff like they were totally expendable – which of course we were!

We actually had a meeting once in which we were told by the MD to put up with abuse from a director because in the end she produced the goods. It was ego city with ridiculous people shouting out things like, 'Don't you know who I am?' The backbiting was unreal as well. It was so cut-throat. One day I was working under massive pressure and someone was recording a porn tape for a programme on sex on a TV next to my desk and I just thought, I can't do this, this is awful. So I resigned.

Although lots of the people I met in that job were brilliant and I had fun too, I generally hated the culture and had no belief in our output. I knew I didn't want to work in light entertainment. And when I thought about going back into more serious TV, I just felt I didn't have the passion to do it. It's fine if you really want it because you can put up with the stress and the job insecurity and there is loads of job satisfaction, variety and fun to be had. But as I wasn't completely passionate about it, I decided I didn't want to do it anymore. I'd watched too many people in their forties and fifties still trying to get their programmes made. I just knew as a career, it was too precarious for me.

WANT TO SEE A TV SHOW BEING RECORDED?

Get tickets from www.beonscreen.com.

REAL LIVES – THE POST-PRODUCTION RUNNER

Brendan Stuart, 24, originally from Lancaster

The job
I've been a runner in a Soho facilities house for six months. The money's terrible and it's hard work, but it's fun and I've never been so fit in all my life. Most of the work that comes through here is a mixture of TV, adverts and music videos. So it's a good learning place for me. I'm staying with my brother and the rent is cheap, otherwise I don't know if I could manage on what I earn. The company I work for is quite small, so they've only got about six edit suites. I've got to pick up tapes around Soho and drop them off, all on foot. I often walk about five miles a day. My job

also entails going and picking up coffees and making toast for the clients and getting them whatever they want from the outside world.

Worst bit
Edit suites are dark, airless places. That can feel a bit depressing in the summer. The hours are really long. If I'm doing the late shift I've got to wait until the last client goes, which can be anything up to midnight and beyond. It is tough and if you didn't want to get on you wouldn't do it. It's basically like going back to school and starting in your first year. I need to laugh, otherwise I could feel like a servant. There are fun creative people in TV and music videos and there are idiots. That means that some people do treat you badly – asking you to warm up their cappuccinos and that kind of thing.

Best bit
A more senior runner here has already started learning to edit and is allowed to use one of the empty suites in her free time. The other runners are fun and all about my age. We have a real good laugh about everything.

Career Ladder

Runner, editing facility in Soho
↑
American Studies at university

TOP TIP

Go to Channel 4's IDEASFACTORY website (www.ideasfactory.com) for inspiration, ideas and master classes. Packed with useful information for anyone trying to get in and get on in the creative industries.

REAL LIVES – THE TV NEWS PRESENTER

Louise Minchin, Presenter, News 24

The job
I present three and a half hours of live evening news in which I usually do numerous live interviews on the main news stories of the day. To do my job you've got to be a perfectionist, inquisitive, quick on the uptake and not panic under pressure. I'm the sort of person who loved exams!

Best bit about the job
I love the fact that it's live and fast moving. At News 24 we're always trying to be first with the news and first with our interviews. It's exciting to be part of that.

Worst bit about the job
I'm the last line of defence, so if something goes wrong I've got to deal with it live on air. It drives me nuts when news stories have been written wrong.

Career path
I started out on work experience at the BBC World Service in 1992. I rang up and organised a placement after university. That meant working free for six weeks, making the tea and getting some hands-on experience. After that I graduated to a paid job as a production assistant for the *Today* programme. I then left the BBC to do a postgraduate course in radio at The London College of Printing. I'd recommend that to anyone – it was excellent. Then I got a job as a reporter on Radio Berkshire.

After two years I moved to News Direct where I worked as a presenter and reporter. Then I got my break into TV reading the news bulletins at Channel Five (now five tv). My next move was to my current presenting job at the BBC. There's been a lot of hard work involved in my career but I've also had the odd lucky break too. I was actually interviewing for a reporter's job at the BBC when they asked me if I could do some presenting on BBC News 24.

Career Ladder

Presenter, BBC News 24
↑
Presenter, Channel Five news
↑
Presenter and reporter, News Direct
↑
Reporter, local radio
↑
Postgraduate radio journalism course, London College of Printing
↑
Production assistant, *Today* programme
↑
Work experience as production assistant, BBC World Service
↑
University degree

LOOK AT ME! I WANT TO BE A PRESENTER!

Most of us who've watched Ant and Dec as they tease celebrities in the jungle or mess around in front of camera on Saturday nights for enormous amounts of money have thought, 'I'd love to do that!' Ant and Dec, two of the most popular presenters on TV, do make it look easy. Budding presenters beware – it's really not. While presenters like Ant and Dec chat to the camera they've got people talking in their ears, they have to take cues and look at the right camera. And often they have to work live. That's why anyone who wants to be a presenter has got to be good under pressure. Getting your first shot at presenting is difficult. But those that make it do so with a mixture of persistence, luck, hard work and being the right face at the right time.

Presenters like Ant and Dec who work in light entertainment often come from a performing background, while news presenters (see Louise Minchin's case study) come from a journalistic background.

Working in production can be a good starting point. Daisy Donovan was picked from the production team of the *11 O'clock News* to front the cult comedy programme.

The light entertainment presenter
Here's the story of a 20-something presenter who was working as a researcher.

'I was working as a researcher in light entertainment documentaries in Anglia TV in Norwich. We were looking for a presenter for a series about buying a house abroad. We couldn't find the right one so I begged them to let me have a go. I did an audition and got the job. It was just being in the right place at the right time. It is also about having the right face. I think I look better on camera than off it!'

JARGON BUSTER

Call sheet – information for a shoot, including the shot list and contact details of everyone taking part. Created by someone in the production team.

REAL LIVES – THE FREELANCE DOCUMENTARY PRODUCER

Jenny Dillon, 33, London

The job
My job entails organising and being creative. I pick the team, run the budget, keep production on schedule, make things happen, find locations, research editorial content and generally make the director's vision happen. I also write scripts and have to generate ideas quickly and find solutions to problems immediately. In production I've got to manage the team, keep them happy and keep production working to time schedules. Because I studied languages at university I often work on programmes that include filming abroad.

Best bit

It is glamorous and it is fun. I travel the world, meet interesting people and work on projects that are constantly new. I never get bored. For each project the subject matter can change massively. I've worked on documentaries on everything from the history of the Mafia and commandos in the Second World War to the Grand Prix and 'killer seaweed'!

Worst bit

As I'm freelance it's incredibly insecure. I never know where I'm going to be next. Budgets are getting smaller and schedules tighter. I have to do double the job I used to because production time is so much shorter. These days you've got to be multi-skilled. On recent productions I've had to do the sound and help lug kit around. In the past I would always have had two people below me. Now often I've got no one to delegate to. A crew going abroad to shoot on location used to be about six or seven people, now it's more likely to be two or four. The really negative thing about being freelance is that there's no holiday pay. Every time a programme finishes I've got to find new work. If you've got overheads, that's stressful. The mortgage keeps coming out of my bank account whether I'm in work or not. Sometimes when I go for a new job I feel like I'm in a giant popularity contest because people don't just hire you on your experience but also on whether they want to work with you.

Career Ladder

Freelance producer in London
↑
Freelance assistant producer in London
↑
Freelance researcher and presenter, documentaries and light entertainment programmes, Anglia TV in Norwich
↑
Freelance researcher, corporate videos for an independent production company in London
↑
Internship at the *Daily Express* newspaper
↑
French and Spanish at university

RELATED OCCUPATIONS

- Advertising

- Film

- Marketing

- Multimedia

- Performing

- Print journalism

- Public relations

- Radio journalism.

CHAPTER 4

Jobs in film

FILM QUIZ

Here's a quick quiz to give you an idea of some of the skills needed to work in film.

1) You're a camera operator, it's late at night and you're still filming. You wish you could get something to eat.

   a) You start thinking about food and drift off so you mess up the shot.
   b) You shout 'Cut' and tell everyone you need food now.
   c) You concentrate and put all your energy into the filming. You love film and want to make sure you get the perfect shot.

2) You're a first assistant director. Some bit-part actors are getting rowdy and disturbing the director who is thinking about the next scene.

   a) You go over and tell them in no uncertain terms to shut up.
   b) You go pink and whisper, 'Can you be quiet, please?'
   c) You figure they will quieten down in a minute.

3) You're an editor on a film with a huge budget. You've spent hours editing and re-editing the same scene.

a) You hate detail. Overall it looks OK. You call it a night.
b) You are a perfectionist bordering on an obsessive. You don't even notice what time it is, you just want to get this section of the film looking perfect.
c) One of the actors/actresses came in earlier to look at some rushes – you got his/her phone number and all you can think about is your forthcoming date.

ANSWERS

1) The correct answer is (c). Being a camera operator requires a massive amount of concentration. You've got to be agile, technically minded and creative.

2) The correct answer is (a). First assistant directors need to keep discipline on set and have to make sure everything goes as smoothly as possible for the director. This job requires strategic thinking as well. You have to be able to see problems before they happen and take steps to overcome them.

3) The correct answer is (b) Editors have to be extremely visual and also technically adept. An essential part of the job is attention to detail. An editor works closely with the director to produce the final film and should be a perfectionist with the ability to focus on tiny sections of the film as well as having a good overall picture of the director's vision.

FASCINATING FACT

Eyes down on set. It is said that some famous actors insert an 'eyes down' clause into their contract. That means that when you pass the actor on set you have to look down. So when you do finally make it on set – no staring! No rubbernecking either!

FILM IN NUMBERS

Around 50,000 people work in the film and video industries in the UK according to the Office of National Statistics Labour Force Survey, Autumn 2002.

Over 25,000 people are studying over 700 media-related courses at over 400 institutions across the UK.

At sixth form in England and Wales there are over 5,000 students studying media-related subjects. Well, there is some point to it all: despite the fact that most people working in the media advise against doing an undergraduate media degree, nearly eight out of ten media graduates find work within six months of graduation compared to nearly seven out of ten of all other graduates[3].

JARGON BUSTER

***Facilities house* – a hub of technical know-how. This is where the editing happens, where the sequence, colour, sound and special effects are born, creating the film from the raw material of the rushes. Editors are crucial to the final product. Some directors edit themselves, while others will oversee the editing process carefully.**

FILM ROLES

CREATORS AND PRODUCTION
These people come up with ideas for a film, develop ideas, put ideas into practice and make them happen.

Roles include:

● **Producer** – develops the original idea, buys the rights, commissions the scriptwriter, finds the director, hires the crew,

[3] *Skills for Tomorrow's Media*, Skillset, 2001; Association of Graduate Careers Advisory Services

manages post-production and lots more. Film producing is a complex creative and managerial job, and the producer has responsibility for the film's ultimate profitability.

- **Director** – uses his or her creative vision to shoot the film; works closely with the producer. This is a highly creative job, and the director must lead a team of creative and technical people to carry out his or her vision.

- **Scriptwriter** – writes and rewrites the film script according to the producer's and director's wishes. Will either be working on his or her idea or be commissioned to fulfil a brief. Likely to have an agent.

- **Production assistant** – helps organise film production, from booking transport to and from set, to producing the daily call sheet. An administrative role.

SKILLED TECHNICAL AND ARTISTIC PEOPLE

Each film is a huge technical undertaking. Working on set will often mean being on location and working flat out. Without the technical and artistic part of the crew the film just wouldn't happen.

Roles include:

- **Director of photography** – uses his/her technical knowledge of lighting and film to create the look the director desires.

- **Costume designer** – dreams up and makes costumes for the actors following a brief.

- **Editor** – cuts the rushes to make the final film. This is a highly significant role. The editor will work closely with the director to shape the film. Some directors come from an editing background.

- **Production designer** – working closely with the costume designers and director of photography, the production designer is head of the art department. He or she works to co-ordinate the film's overall look and come in on budget.

- **Clapper loader** – assists camera operators, including loading and unloading film, looking after the camera equipment and working the clapperboard.

BUSINESS AND FINANCE

Film is a multi-million dollar business and there are plenty of jobs related to finance, publicity and distribution.

Roles include:

- **Production accountant** – manages the film's budget and controls the spend during production. Must be organised, good with figures and good under pressure.

- **Film PR** – promoting the film during the cinema and DVD/video release dates.

> For more information on specific jobs in film, read *Creative Careers: Film* by Milly Jenkins, published by Trotman.

ENTRY-LEVEL JOBS

There are a few ways into film. You could be like Quentin Tarantino and write an amazing script that gets picked up; or become a hugely bankable star like Robert Redford and then move into directing. Or, much more realistically, you can work your way up from the bottom.

We've all got to start somewhere. Think Martin Scorsese, Steven Spielberg, Pedro Almodóvar, Jane Campion – inspiring names. But I bet at one time or other in their careers they've made the tea and worked themselves silly for little money or thanks. Film is a highly technical business, and useful technical skills will always help you progress up the career ladder. Whatever you start out as, keep your eyes and ears open. Remember, you need to learn everything you can to get on. Listen to advice and be keen.

However, you are a human being. Be diplomatic but don't let anyone push you too far.

Entry-level jobs include:

- Runner
- Production Assistant
- Clapper Loader/Camera Assistant
- Sound Assistant
- Lighting Assistant
- Third Assistant Director
- Art Department Assistant

- Wardrobe Assistant
- Make-up/Hair Assistant
- Props Assistant
- Post-Production Runner/Assistant Editor
- Casting Assistant
- Assistant Location Manager

CASH

Like TV, film can be an incredibly lucrative business, but not usually when you're starting out. Most runners and other entry-levels jobs are paid at extremely low rates. Start developing a taste for tuna sandwiches.

The following are the minimum rates agreed in the Freelance Production Agreement. as agreed by BECTU, the largest broadcasters union and PACT, the Producer's Alliance for Cinema and Television.

Weekly Rates

	40-hour week	72-hour week
Art Department Assistant, Technical Assistant	£251	£552

Production Secretary, Third Assistant Director	£281	£618
Clapper Loader, Junior Make-up/ Hair Assistant, Publicity Assistant	£375	£825
Sound Assistant, Graphic Artist, Assistant Script Supervisor	£389	£855
Wardrobe Assistant, Props Person, Assistant Editor	£430	£946
Dubbing Editor, Production Co-ordinator, Third Assistant Director	£455	£1,000
Boom Operator, Location Manager, Focus Puller, Grip	£496	£1,092
Production Buyer, Set Decorator, Unit Publicist	£528	£1,160
Camera Operator, Art Director	£570	£1,254
Editor, Production Accountant, Construction Manager, Costume	£644	£1,417

Movies on a shoestring

You don't have to be an expert to make a film. If you're a budding film director, don't just talk about it, start now. You don't have to spend millions to make a great film. Jonathan Caouette spent just £124 making his film *Tarnation*. An autobiographical documentary, the film was so well received at the 2004 Cannes Film Festival it earned him a standing ovation. The 31-year-old director had started filming his life experiences at the age of 11. The film provides an honest and heart-wrenching portrayal of the director's difficult life. Be inspired by all the films at the Cannes Film Festival. See www.festival-cannes.fr.

Cutting Edge

See as many new films as possible – not just at the cinema. The Sheffield International Documentary Film Festival is where all the aficionados can be seen checking out the latest talent in documentary film making and factual TV (www.sidf.co.uk).

REAL LIVES – THE PRODUCTION ASSISTANT

Kate Cheswick, 22, Leeds

The job

I assist the production co-ordinator and the producer during the pre-production stage and filming. My role is mainly straightforward administration. I deal with phone calls, queries, produce daily call sheets and assist the production co-ordinator in booking cars to get all the people to the right places. I also make sure everyone's got the right version of the script. I'm involved in booking sparks (electricians) and I liaise with the agencies that hold information about all the freelance contributors to a film. These agencies are called diary services and hold the diaries of everyone from freelance technicians to freelance people in the art department. You can ring up and ask for a particular person and they'll tell you if they're free on the day you want them. They will also recommend people for specific jobs.

Best bit

It's a great place to be if you want to become a producer or part of the production team that puts together a movie. I work closely with the production co-ordinator and producer. It's also a good position from which to learn about all the different people on film and what jobs they do. It's one step up from being a production runner. If you want to be a director you'd be better off trying to get a job as a floor runner. As a production assistant I hardly ever make it to the floor to see the filming taking place. However, floor runners are hard jobs to get – production assistant jobs are probably easier. To be a production assistant, you need good computer and organisational skills and bags of enthusiasm. It is low pay. I have been paid as little as £50 a day.

I'm usually on a daily or weekly rate. If the production office is on location, you go wherever filming is taking place.

Worst bit
The job is totally dependent on your relationship with the production co-ordinator and the producer. If they're big shouters it can be quite hard. Hours are long and when you're working it's likely to be seven days a week. Like a runner, the production assistant is the first into work in the morning and the last to go at night. Also, even though you're no longer a runner, you may get asked to do a runner's job like get the sandwiches and coffees. Basically you're bottom of the pile. In my case I was lucky. I formed a good relationship with a production co-ordinator. As soon as she became a producer she took me with her as a production assistant on her next jobs.

Best bit
Everybody comes into the production office so you meet everyone. Films are quite gossipy and in the production office you get to hear about everything that's happening. It's really interesting seeing how the budget works and it's satisfying seeing all the organising you've done coming together – like when all the people you've booked turn up.

Career path
I studied English at Leeds University. While I was there I volunteered at film schools in Leeds and worked on student productions for free. After university I got a job in a TV drama as a runner, then became a runner on a film and then a production assistant on a film.

```
Career Ladder

Production assistant on film
↑
Runner on film
↑
Runner on TV drama
↑
Runner on student films
↑
English at university
```

JARGON BUSTER

Sculpture and animatronics. **Ever seen** *Godzilla*? **This is a branch of film visual effects specialising in large-scale scary looking things. Britain has a fantastic reputation for its visual effects specialists.**

REAL LIVES – THE ASSISTANT CASTING DIRECTOR

Gillian Edmunds, 26, London

The job

The job is choosing the right actors and actresses for specific productions in film and TV. I assisted an independent casting director. People came to us to find actors for big productions. As an assistant casting director my job was to constantly look out for new actors.

To work in casting you need to know all the faces out there – not just Julia Roberts! You've got to be imaginative and have a good eye for faces. You've got to constantly spot new talent. That means you have to be pretty dedicated, looking out for bit-part actors with some flair and going to student productions and end-of-year shows.

Forging good relationships with key agents is also important. Agents can be very difficult. For example, sometimes they will tell you that their client can't read a script that you want them to read for. That's a way of hyping the actor to make them look really busy.

You've got to have good people skills and be polite and courteous. It's not for the faint-hearted. Actors come in and tell you their life story and it feels awful when they are rejected for the job. In the end, with the amount of auditions you see, most actors are rejected. I just found that really depressing so I decided it wasn't for me.

FASCINATING FACTS

Directors' favourite directors

Orson Welles	Billy Wilder
Federico Fellini	Ingmar Bergman
Akira Kurosawa	Martin Scorsese
Francis Ford Coppola	David Lean
Alfred Hitchcock	Jean Renoir
Stanley Kubrick	

Source: *Sight and Sound* (see www.bfi.org.uk/sightandsound)

REAL LIVES – THE SCRIPT EDITOR/DEVELOPMENT EXECUTIVE

Elizabeth Edmunds

The job

The job is working with the producer to find good stories that will make great films. You are looking to commission a writer to develop an idea or to find a writer's story to turn into a film. You source material from everywhere, from the Internet to newspaper articles and magazines. Spotting new writing talent is a vital part of the job. I keep in touch with all the publishing houses. You have to find the best novels first, in case your producer wants to buy the 'option'. That means you buy the rights to turn a book into a film. You need to be quite sociable as you've got to talk to all the agents to find out about their scriptwriters and keep abreast of who's the best and who the new ones are. The job is fun but it does start to take over your life. I go everywhere to spot talent, to fringe theatre, live comedy and festivals like Edinburgh and Spitalfields. And it's not just writers I'm looking for, another part of the job is spotting the up-and-coming directors from TV and film. For example, the director who did the famous Guinness advert with the horses and the waves went on to direct *Sexy Beast*. It's my job to find the perfect project and help put the perfect team together to make a fantastic film.

It's a great role if you want to become a film producer. Basically, you're learning the producer's job – only you've got nothing to do with the money. But you have to be aware of how much things cost in order to get the ingredients right. If you've found a good first-time director you're unlikely to give him a script that's cost a million pounds – it's too risky. So for a first-time director you've got to find an affordable writer who matches the scale of the proposition you're entering. When choosing scriptwriters you're paid for your opinions on the quality of the writing. The producer has the ultimate decision, but you give your opinion.

Once the producer has chosen a writer for a project, he or she is commissioned to write a script. There are usually then a few rewrites. Each time I read the script and write my script notes for the producer. My notes comment on the technical aspects of the script – like its structure and pace. Then the producer reads the script and gives feedback to the writer. Often as a script editor I'm involved in these meetings. The key is to be incredibly diplomatic because the writer's ego is fragile. You will probably have to get him or her back three or four times for rewrites. Let's say you pay a writer somewhere between £30,000 and £1,000,000 – you've got to keep them on board because you're going to need rewrites maybe even up to the last day. If they walk off the project, that's a disaster. As a script editor you also have a hand in helping the producer cast the film, in that you make suggestions for the casting. At some point during this process the director comes on board.

Best bit
It's a really creative process. I love meeting the writers and helping develop an idea from a seed to the finish. It's fantastic and when the film's complete, there's a screening with cast and crew. That's the best bit!

Worst bit
I don't get any credit. The producer takes all the credit for whatever I do.

Career Ladder

Script Editor
↑
Trainee Script Editor, Granada
↑
Assistant at ICM (International Creative Management), UK's
leading agents for directors, writers and actors
↑
Production secretary at a live events TV production
company
↑
Production secretary, BBC documentary
↑
English at university

RELATED OCCUPATIONS

● Advertising

● Marketing

● Multimedia

● Performing

● Print journalism

● Public relations

● Radio journalism

● TV.

CHAPTER 5

Jobs in radio

RADIO QUIZ

Here's a quick quiz to give you an idea of some of the skills needed to work in radio.

1) After sending off loads of CVs, you get offered low-paid work experience on local radio. You've done a week and it's been tough going.

a) You decide to pack it in. You're being underpaid anyway.
b) You go into work and make a huge fuss that you want to be treated like someone special – after all, you're giving up your free time.
c) You keep going back and focus on what you can learn from the experience.

2) You're the studio manager on a live breakfast show. You are responsible for the output of the programme. A technical hitch means you've played a jingle at the wrong time.

a) You keep calm, sort it out and go on to the next thing.
b) You run out of the studio in shame.

c) You hate pressure and wish you had a different job.

3) **A meeting is called to come up with ideas for a new celebrity slot on the national music radio station at which you're a production assistant.**

a) You just want to be told what to do so you can get on with it. You try and get out of the meeting.
b) This is your big chance – you can't wait to shine in the meeting. You've got so many ideas you don't know which ones to share.
c) You've got masses of administration to do and you just feel bogged down so you can't be bothered to waste your time.

ANSWERS

1) The correct answer is (c). To get on in radio you've got to be persistent – you can't give up at the first hurdle. Work experience depends very much on who you're working for. You could be assigned to making the tea for days on end. But you have to get the best out of it. Be polite, enthusiastic and interested in radio. Make the tea but also ask radio-related questions. Ask if you can help out in any other way. You have to be diplomatic. You can always learn something from any situation. Remember, everyone there will probably have done low-paid bottom-rung work – they won't want to hear you whingeing about it.

2) The correct answer is (a). The studio manager has to be able to keep calm under pressure and foresee and correct any problems. He or she also has to keep an ear out for any possible legal problems – interviewees may say something slanderous, for example.

3) The correct answer is (b). Most non-technical roles in radio require you to be an ideas person. Good broadcasting thrives on constant creativity. It's a fun part of the job. Ideas and writing skills are seen as essentials for non-technical jobs in radio.

JARGON BUSTER

RCS Master Control – most of the radio industry has now gone digital and uses hard disk play-out systems like RCS Master Control. Go to www.rcuk.com to find out more.

RADIO OVERVIEW

With so many different TV channels out there, you might think radio was a thing of the past. Far from it! Ninety-one per cent of adults listen to radio every day and the average listening time is three-and-a-half hours, according to the *2003 Guardian Media Guide*. There are 310 official radio stations, 50 of which are part of the BBC (see *Creative Careers: Radio* by Tania Shillam, published by Trotman).

Radio can be broken down into the following categories:

● Music

● News

● Sport

● Talk

● Drama

● Magazine programmes.

CREATORS AND PRODUCTION

This includes jobs such as:

● **Presenter** – researches stories, does interviews and sometimes 'drives' the desk (i.e. is responsible for sound output, including jingles and music). Presenters of news programmes are likely to come from a journalistic background.

- **Radio production assistant** – this is a great place to start to find out about the industry. The role is basically administrative. You could be doing anything from typing up scripts to answering the phone or checking details to responding to listeners' letters and emails. This role is hands on and in the thick of things.

- **Broadcast assistant** – in this role you can start learning broadcast and technical skills. Administrative tasks are involved but you are also likely to be involved in research and production.

- **Producer** – a role for a creative and organised person. The producer comes up with programme ideas, handles the budget and oversees production.

TECHNICAL

This area includes jobs such as **technical operator/studio producer**, who makes the sound output possible. In live radio a studio operator manages all the technical aspects of radio transmissions. When radio is not live but pre-recorded this person records, edits and mixes the audio.

JARGON BUSTER

Sound editing packages **– these are used to edit sound in the studios. You can get these packages for your PC and turn it into a recording studio. Cool Edit Pro and Pro Tools are both commonly used in the workplace. Packages can be downloaded for free on the Internet.**

CASH

As with other media jobs, starting salaries are not particularly high. According to the Prospects graduate recruitment website you can expect to be paid the following in these radio production jobs. Popular presenters, like Johnny Vaughn, competing on a high-profile breakfast slot command considerably higher fees!

- Broadcast assistant – £11,000–£22,000 a year

- Radio producer – £15,000–£22,000 a year.

JARGON BUSTER

Mixing desk – produces the sound output and includes faders and monitors.

REAL LIVES – THE RADIO DJ

Bali Deol, 21, originally from Huddersfield, is a presenter on Awaz FM 107.2 Community Radio, Glasgow

The job
I present my own show at drive-time and do an R&B top ten. Presenting isn't just about talking! It also includes lots of research. I've got to interview people on the show so a lot of background work goes into that. I've just finished my degree in media, theory and production at Paisley University. It included a mix of theory and practical stuff. We did everything from advertising to radio production and journalism. I also considered doing the media course at Caledonian but I chose the Paisley course because it was more hands on. I'm glad I did, as I really enjoyed it and I've found the practical skills I learned useful in this job.

Best bit
I feel passionate about broadcasting. I've always wanted to work in radio and TV. My show is a mixture of R&B, bhangra and hip hop. It's music I love and the job allows me to be how I am. I'm quite an extrovert and presenting is a perfect job for that.

Worst bit
The research can get boring because it's demanding.

Career path
While I was at university a friend of mine was doing a show on Awaz on Friday night. He asked me if I wanted to do it with him.

It worked really well and we had a lot of fun and the show had energy and was popular. After that I got a joint presenting slot on drive-time and then I got my own show.

Career Ladder

Presenter on community radio
↑
Co-presenter on community radio
↑
Media, theory and production at Paisley University

TOP TIP

Go to the Radio Academy website at www.radioacademy.org/gettingin where they have a fantastic guide to getting into radio with tips from the great and the good in the industry, including John Peel.

JARGON BUSTER

***Driving a desk* means the same as operating the mixing desk in the radio studio.**

For more information go to www.prospects.ac.uk/links/occupations, www.bbc.co.uk, Channel 4's creative career site, www.ideasfactory.com/careers/index.htm or the Skillsformedia site at www.skillsformedia.com.

REAL LIVES – THE RADIO RESEARCHER

Michael Smith, 23

Career path
I went to Manchester University and did a history degree. After university I got a place at Cardiff to do a postgraduate broadcast

diploma. It's one of the best places to do a journalism course, so I was thrilled. The group interview to get in was a bit gruelling but it was worth it. During my year at Cardiff I got good practical experience. I was taught how to write for broadcast and how to use the equipment. I decided I didn't want to be a reporter but wanted to work on magazine programmes and documentaries rather than rolling news.

While I was doing my course I got a part-time job in BBC Radio Wales. My part-time job was two mornings a week. I got up at 5am and did a lowly job downloading news stories for local stations. It was tiring but a really good thing to do. As part of the course I also visited lots of different radio stations from local stations to the BBC.

The work experience I did as part of my course was perfect for what I wanted to do. It was in a department of the BBC in London that makes current affairs programmes for TV and radio. When my work experience finished, I was hired for six weeks to work as a researcher on a new discussion programme on Radio 4 and then I went from contract to contract with contracts getting longer.

Best bit
I enjoy covering so many interesting subjects. I've researched everything from health and crime to the economy. I've worked with loads of presenters which is always quite good fun. The other satisfying part of the job is that it's quite independent, to a large extent I'm left to my own devices to come up with information and ideas.

Worst bit
Speech radio is a small world. There aren't many places to work. If things don't work out at the BBC there are some small independent production companies but it's difficult to get staff jobs anywhere.

I'm thinking of leaving and trying to work in print journalism as well. Although I love the work, I feel I need another form of journalism as a back up. Working in radio documentaries feels precarious as it's mostly freelance and there's not much you can do if they don't want to renew your contract.

Career Ladder

Freelance researcher, Radio 4
↑
Work experience, Radio 4
↑
Part-time job, BBC Wales
↑
MA in Broadcast Journalism, Cardiff Centre for Journalism
↑
History at university

RELATED OCCUPATIONS

● Advertising

● Film

● Marketing

● Multimedia

● Performing

● Print journalism

● Public relations

● TV journalism.

CHAPTER 6

Newspapers and magazines

NEWSPAPERS AND MAGAZINES QUIZ

Here's a quick quiz to give you an idea of some of the skills needed to work in newspapers and magazines.

1) You are offered a junior writer's job on a current affairs magazine.

   a) Great! You're a news junkie. You read papers, watch news and keep up to date with world affairs – this is your dream job.
   b) Kofi who?
   c) Yawn – I always switch over when the news is on.

2) You're a journalist working in a press agency specialising in financial journalism. Your editor doesn't like your story. She gives it back to you, tells you in no uncertain terms what she thinks of it and screams you've got to rewrite your 600 words in half an hour. You're on a deadline for a national newspaper – the features desks need your story now.

a) You say 'I can't do it' and burst into tears.
b) You ask the editor to be specific about what extras and changes she wants and knuckle down and do it.
c) You say it's a boring story and you can't be bothered to rewrite it, get your coat and go home.

3) You're doing a feature on a big soap star for a women's magazine. The soap star is also going to be on the cover. When you arrive to interview her she is incredibly rude to you.

a) You say, 'Stuff your interview – I'm not being spoken to like that'.
b) You punch her in the face and walk out.
c) You are diplomatic and try to win her over. There's no way you're leaving without your story and that's that.

ANSWERS

1) The correct answer is of course (a). There are magazines about everything. Use your interests to help you get on. Gravitate towards what fascinates you. This will not only help you to enjoy your job but will also help you to be good at it.

2) The correct answer is (b). There will be times in newspaper journalism when you are so stressed you think you will explode. But you have to make deadlines and give the editor what he or she wants. You can't be too touchy if your work is criticised.

3) The correct answer is (c). You're not the star, you're the journalist. You've got to get your story. Diplomacy is a large part of the job. Someone at the magazine, if not you, will have worked hard to secure a big interview and no one will accept you coming back without a complete interview.

JARGON BUSTER

Copy. **The journalist's text is referred to as copy, as in 'Hurry up with that copy! The features desk needs it now!'**

JOBS IN NEWSPAPERS AND MAGAZINES

EDITORIAL AND DESIGN

Writers, editors and designers work together to create stimulating, attention-grabbing and accurate content for newspapers and magazines. Once content has been researched and written, it must be checked, altered if necessary to make it adhere to a consistent 'house style' and made to fit the page. Many newspapers and magazines have now branched out into other media and include an interactive online site.

Jobs in this area include:

- **Editor** – edits final content, decides on the overall content and ultimately takes responsibility for those decisions. When Piers Morgan, former editor of the *Mirror*, recently took the decision to print photographs of Iraqi prisoners being mistreated that were later found to be fake, he was sacked.

- **Sub-editor** – checks and rewrites copy written by journalists before it's laid out on the page. All copy must be put into 'house style' by the sub and checked for potential legal problems. In some cases the sub-editor will also design and lay out the pages.

- **Magazine journalist** – generates and researches ideas, carries out interviews and writes copy. On smaller magazines writers may be involved in many other parts of the magazine process including sub-editing and layout.

- **Newspaper journalist** – reports the news and writes features on everything from current affairs to fashion. Writing skills, tenacity and attention to detail are essential.

BUSINESS AND FINANCE

Newspapers and magazines are big business and profit is driven by sales and advertising revenue, aided by marketing and advertising sales (the revenue created from companies paying to advertise in the publication).

Jobs in advertising sales involve securing lucrative adverts on the pages of a publication. To succeed at this job you have to have drive and enjoy working with targets in a pressurised environment.

For more information on working in magazines and newspapers go to the Prospects website, at www.prospects.ac.uk.

For more information on working on local newspapers go to www.newspapersoc.org.uk.

TOP TIP

Magazine and newspaper journalists often become specialists in an area, anything from health to technology. This can help career advancement and helps freelancers to get work.

CASH[4]

● **A sub-editor** on a local paper or small magazine earns somewhere between **£12,000** and **£15,000**. On a larger regional this rises to around **£17,000** and a chief sub-editor on a national can earn **£50,000** plus.

● **A magazine journalist** just starting out is likely to be earning around **£10,000** to **£15,000**. As his or her career progresses the money will go up to around **£20,000** to **£50,000** plus.

● **A newspaper journalist** training on a local newspaper will earn somewhere between **£11,000** and **£14,000**. At more senior level, depending on the size of the publication and profile of the journalist, salaries range from **£20,000** to **£100,000** plus. There is huge money available if you make it big!

[4] Figures from Prospects website (www.prospects.ac.uk)

REAL LIVES – THE SENIOR REPORTER ON A LOCAL NEWSPAPER

Simon Conlan, 25, Manchester

The job

Every week I do about four lead articles of 400 words, then three or four second lead articles of maybe 300 words and then eight fillers which is maybe 120 words and then five or six NIBS – news in briefs which are around 50 words. And you spend a lot of time on the phone researching stories and going out and about meeting people. We work 9am–5.30pm but you tend to work a bit later most nights, and occasionally you might have a night meeting.

Career path

I started as a trainee reporter. I got the job after my pre-entry exams at the end of my journalism course. After 18 months as a trainee you sit your final exams and if you pass those, you're a qualified senior reporter. Now I'm thinking about what to do next. I could stay at this local paper and hope to get a chief reporter's job. If I take that route I'll take on more management functions, stop writing so much and start editing other people's work with a view to becoming an editor of my paper. The other option is to move to a trade magazine or to move to a regional daily like the *Manchester Evening News* or the *Birmingham Evening Post*. I think I might try a trade magazine as then I could become an expert in an area like health or technology and then move to a national. To get on to a national newspaper directly from a local, I would have needed to try to sell some stories while I was working here or get weekend shifts on a national newspaper. To make the local to national leap, you've got to be hugely ambitious and not want any free time. I was having too much fun to do that!

Best bit

I like the variety. I cover everything from crime, planning and community to transport and local politics – as long as it's on my patch. I enjoy writing. It's great to see your name in print at the end of the week. They're a nice bunch of people at my paper and there's a culture of going out and having fun after all the hard work is done. Most people tend to be quite young – early to mid-twenties. There are a few exceptions as some people come to it older. There are eight of us on my paper, six reporters, a chief and a news editor. In our office there's four different newspapers. So there's lots of opportunity to meet interesting people.

Worst bit

Pay is bad on local papers. Even in London trainees only get something like £14,000 a year. That's for a graduate with a postgraduate journalism qualification. There's also something called a death knock, which I think is the worst part of the job. Luckily I haven't had to do too many of these. A death knock is when someone from your paper's area dies in an unusual way and your editor sends you out to get a comment from their nearest relations. That's obviously horrible and no one likes doing it. Once I had to track down the mother of a murdered teenager, go to her house, and ask her for her side of the story. It can feel like you're really invading people's privacy. The job can be quite stressful. Sometimes you feel the deadlines are good as there's a bit of adrenaline going. Other times, if you've got three or four stories to write, and you're under pressure, it can feel a bit much. I'd say you have to like pressure if you want to go into news reporting. Newspapers work on pressure.

Career Ladder

Senior reporter, local newspaper
↑
Trainee reporter, local newspaper
↑
Postgraduate journalism course
↑
Politics and Sociology at university

JARGON BUSTER

News – as opposed to features, which are more analytical, news has to be about something new to readers – otherwise it isn't news!

REAL LIVES – EDITOR OF *THE WEEK* MAGAZINE

Caroline Law, 32, London

Best bit
It's an easy-going office, the work is interesting, and it's well paid. It's also nice to be in charge.

Worst bit
The long hours, and having to work at weekends. I spend hours on Saturdays and Sundays wading through the papers.

Career path
After university I went into publishing but ended up working on business books, which I found deeply boring. After two years, I was so fed up I jacked it in and took a 50 per cent pay cut to work as an office dogsbody at *The Oldie* magazine. My title was Editorial Assistant. I was there for two years, during which time I was promoted to sub-editor/assistant editor. It's a small magazine so I was able to move up the ranks quickly. I then moved to *The Week* as a junior writer/assistant editor. That was five years ago. I was made deputy editor and then became editor last September.

The job
As editor I decide the content of the magazine and make sure all the copy is up to the finished standard. I do some of the writing myself, but also have to spend time re-writing inadequate copy and making decisions about pictures, headlines and captions. I manage the editorial team, and am responsible for making sure we keep within budgets. I spend a lot of time discussing the final content with other editorial staff – it's not an autocracy – and deciding things like the cover image. From time to time, I have meetings with the advertising team to discuss ideas for maximising revenue.

Career Ladder

Editor at *The Week* magazine
↑
Deputy editor at *The Week* magazine
↑
Assistant editor at *The Week* magazine
↑
Assistant editor at *The Oldie* magazine
↑
Editorial assistant at *The Oldie* magazine
↑
Business publishing
↑
Law at university

To be fully informed on up-to-the-minute news, read the BBC and Guardian websites every day at www.bbc.co.uk and www.guardian.co.uk.

REAL LIVES – THE NATIONAL NEWSPAPER PICTURE EDITOR

Dave White, 36, London

The job
It's divided mainly into two areas. Firstly, I commission photographers: assign them jobs and set up those jobs. You've got to be properly briefed (normally by section editors) so you know what is needed for the story and be able to pass that on to your chosen photographer. The other side of the job is researching pictures, usually with picture agencies. For example, if someone is doing an interview with Margaret Thatcher, you need to commission a new photograph of her and also find historical images relevant to the story.

Best bit
It's a very creative job and if you get a newspaper that appreciates photography, your job is as creative as the writer who is telling the story.

Worst bit

It can be a very high-pressure environment and you have to meet deadlines. If you are a person who doesn't like to work at a frenetic pace, a newspaper might not be for you. The job of picture editing in a magazine is less frenetic as you've got longer to make decisions.

Career path

I went to university and did an unrelated degree. While I was a student I did a lot of photography as a hobby. After I graduated I got an internship at Polaroid, then went to work for a photography gallery. My next move was to work on the picture desks of a fashion magazine and then a travel magazine. Finally, I moved to a national newspaper and became deputy picture editor and then eventually became picture editor.

Career Ladder

Picture editor, a national newspaper
↑
Deputy picture editor, a national newspaper
↑
Picture desk, a travel magazine
↑
Picture desk, a fashion magazine
↑
Assistant, photography gallery
↑
Internship, Polaroid
↑
University degree

JARGON BUSTER

The clothesline intro – so named because you can hang everything on it. A style of news reporting in which the introduction includes six questions – who, what, how, where, when and why.

REAL LIVES – THE NEWS AGENCY REPORTER

Fiona Chadwick, 34, originally from Stirling, now living in London

I studied languages at university and after that joined a local newspaper. From the local newspaper I got a job with the news agency.

The job
I cover the oil markets. I report on all the news related to global oil markets.

Best bit
I've had my stories printed all over the world. It's good money. Also, the agency I work for has offices across the world. So there's always the possibility of securing a post abroad.

Worst bit
Covering one area can get a bit repetitive. The hours are long. And I spend a lot of my time talking to traders to find out what's going on. Sometimes they can be irritating.

Career Ladder

News agency reporter
↑
Local newspaper reporter
↑
Languages at university

RELATED OCCUPATIONS

- Advertising

- Film

- Marketing

- Multimedia

- Performing

- Public relations

- Radio journalism

- TV.

CHAPTER 7

Books and publishing

BOOKS AND PUBLISHING QUIZ

Here's a quick quiz to give you an idea of some of the skills needed to work in books and publishing.

1) You work in the marketing department of a book publishers. You are asked to give a presentation on anticipated sales figures for a particular series of books.

    a) You're good with numbers so you calculate your targets and explain how you've arrived at them.
    b) You're terrified of numbers and beg one of your colleagues to do the presentation for you.
    c) You blag it and just spew some numbers off the top of your head.

2) You're an editorial assistant. A new Internet site has been set up relating to an educational book that has just been published. Your boss asks you to check through the copy for errors.

a) You have a quick look and miss quite a few mistakes. You're a big picture person.
b) You have an acute eye for detail. You home in on misused possessive apostrophes like a hawk.
c) You'd rather write the copy than read through it.

3) **You're the production director. It's your job to make sure your books and products are produced as cheaply as possible. You enter into negotiations with your paper supplier.**

a) You're a killer negotiator. You get your company the lowest price ever for paper.
b) You feel sorry for the paper supplier. He's always been so nice, you just don't have the heart to ask him to rethink his price.
c) The supplier takes you out to lunch and gets you drunk – you agree to pay more for paper.

ANSWERS

1) The correct answer is of course (a). A lot of sales and marketing jobs require you to be numerate. Marketing departments have to anticipate demand correctly. If they get the numbers wrong it can be a costly mistake.

2) The correct answer is (b). Most editorial work requires you to be good at detail.

3) The correct answer is (a). As a production director you've got to be a brilliant negotiator. Production is all about producing a quality product at the lowest possible cost. It's essential that the company's bottom line is your priority.

PUBLISHING OVERVIEW

The good news is that Britain is a European publishing hotspot. We have the second largest publishing industry in Europe.

The UK publishing industry turns over at least £18.4 billion every year and employs around 164,000 people, according to the DTI.

The majority of employment is in London, with one-third of publishing jobs. Around a fifth of jobs are in the South East[5].

Publishing is known for its long hours and relatively low pay. But if you love books there's no greater industry to be in. Unfortunately you should forget any fantasy notions of publishing you may have in which book lovers take long lunches discussing their favourite authors. The modern publishing business is driven by financial return. Many people working in publishing will tell you the hours are long, work is stressful and costs are increasingly kept down. The financial rewards for working in publishing are not high when compared to many other graduate careers.

FASCINATING FACT

Growth area: according to the Publishing Association the estimated UK retail sales of children's books went up from £245 million in 1990 to £289 million in 1999.

AVERAGE SALARY BY LOCATION

Central London	£23,649
Greater London	£23,267
North England	£21,805
Midlands and East Anglia	£22,253
South and South East England	£21,724
South West England	£19,090
Wales	£25,500
Scotland	£18,808
Ireland	£20,050

Source: Bookcareers.com 2002. For latest figures and more information, go to Bookcareers.com

FASCINATING FACT

There were 125,390 new books published in the UK in 2002, according to the Publishers Association.

[5] Prospects website (www.prospects.ac.uk)

JOBS IN PUBLISHING

You could work in any of the following areas:

- General or consumer

- Children's

- Educational, academic and specialist (including medical, business, etc.)

PUBLISHING FUNCTIONS

According to the Publishers Association, publishing functions are broken down into the following areas.

- **Editorial** – researching, writing and editing texts.

- **Design and production** – creating the look of the pages and producing the product for the printer.

- **Marketing, sales and publicity** – generating sales and calculating product demand.

- **Distribution** – supplying demand, including invoicing and stock control.

- **Rights and contracts** – dealing with authors' and publishers' rights in the national and international market.

- **Finance and administration** – dealing with finance matters including payroll and authors' royalties.

TOP TIP

Finance and accounting jobs can lead to senior management positions in publishing. Go to the Publishers Association website, www.publishers.org.uk, to find out more.

EDITORIAL

Jobs in this area are highly sought-after and this is probably the most difficult area in publishing to break into. A good entry-level job is an editorial assistant. These positions are not easy to secure. However, work experience, demonstrable passion for books and persistence can help. A publishing qualification is also useful, although not essential.

Jobs in this area include:

- **Commissioning editor** – decides what to publish. In a niche publisher, such as a careers publisher, the commissioning editor is likely to be an expert in the publishers' specialist area.

- **Reader** – assesses unsolicited manuscripts.

- **Copy-editor** – corrects errors of grammar, punctuation, spelling and meaning. A detail-focused job.

- **Editorial assistant** – assists senior editorial staff and learns basic skills related to commissioning, planning and production.

JARGON BUSTER

Slush pile – unsolicited manuscripts sent in by authors direct to publishers. Most commissioning editors prefer authors who already have agents.

DESIGN AND PRODUCTION

This includes jobs such as:

- **Head of production** – a senior management role, managing the people in the production department. He or she is ultimately responsible for keeping costs down and maintaining a financially successful and productive department.

● **Print manager** (aka print supervisor or production planner) – ensures print deadlines are met, oversees department and checks the quality of the product.

● **Production manager** – manages the production team to ensure a good quality product is delivered to the printers on time and in budget.

● **Book designer** – works to a brief to create the look of a book. This is likely to include typeface, type size and cover illustration (although the latter may be commissioned from an illustrator by the designer). Increasingly designers in publishing will also work in multimedia, including CDs and websites.

To work in production you need to be organised and numerate, as the ability to keep a tight control of scheduling and costs is essential at all levels. To be a designer you will need artistic flair and training.

CASH

AVERAGE SALARY BY JOB TITLE

	2002	2001
Editorial Assistant	£15,437	£15,329
Editorial Secretary	£15,196	£16,933
Production Assistant	£15,492	£15,920
Rights Assistant	£15,910	£14,271
Sales and Marketing Assistant	£14,132	£15,500
Sales Assistant	£16,053	£15,075
Assistant Editor	£17,618	£16,398
Production Editor	£18,361	£18,565
Production Controller	£19,307	£19,381
Desk Editor	£18,289	£16,917
Managing Editor	£24,835	£23,891
Commissioning Editor	£24,553	£25,084
Marketing Co-ordinator	£17,217	£17,096

Marketing Executive	£20,189	£19,327
Sales Representative	£23,439	£21,683
Marketing Manager	£27,467	£25,641
Publicity Manager	£23,897	£23,117
Rights Manager	£23,770	£25,374
Sales Manager	£29,202	£28,137
Production Manager	£28,631	£26,281
Publisher	£36,368	£37,289
Sales and Marketing Director	£59,200	£45,345
Marketing Director	£41,571	£43,044
Editorial Director	£38,225	£39,750

Source: Bookcareers.com Survey 2002

JARGON BUSTER

Backlist – no, it's not a list written on your back! A publisher's backlist is the list of their previously published books. A publisher's backlist is an important source of revenue, because backlist sales are more predictable and dependable than frontlist (new book) sales.

REAL LIVES – THE COMMISSIONING EDITOR

Julia Moffatt, ex-commissioning editor at Scholastic Children's Books, now a freelance editor and author

The job

A commissioning editor looks for new books to publish. In my case these came from three sources. First, from our existing authors who came to me with new ideas. Second, I would come up with ideas for series; and third, agents would send in the work of authors new to Scholastic. The bit I loved was having the idea for a series and then finding the right author to fulfil the commission. Developing an idea with an author can be quite a mutual process. I commissioned the Point Crime series, for example, and that was great fun to work on. Finding the right author for an idea is a case of matching the writer's style with the concept. I once considered a famous author for the Point

Crime series – obviously before she was as famous as she is now. At the time I didn't think she was right for the series, although I could see she was a wonderful writer.

Dealing with agents is another part of the job. Although some famous authors have been found in the slush pile (see above) I never found any new authors that way, so I would usually turn to agents for new authors. I would send a brief out to agents with what we were looking for. Having said that, occasionally the agents would ignore the brief and just send in whatever they wanted! And sometimes I found a great new author that way.

The final stage is when you take the finished product to the sales conference where you try to sell your list of books to hard-bitten reps. That can be nerve-wracking. I enjoy public speaking, so I always tried to make them laugh while getting the salient points across. There's definitely a bit of pain and pleasure involved in that part of the job!

Best bit
I really did love my job. Having ideas was definitely my favourite part. I used to love the energy involved in bringing an idea to fruition. It's really satisfying choosing the cover and seeing the finished work. One author I enjoyed working with was Susan Price. Her book, *The Sterkarm Handshake*, won the Guardian award for children's fiction in 1998 and it deserved it. It's a fantastic book, a fantasy involving time travel with a wonderful love story. She's just a brilliant author to work with. When you have a fantastic author like Susan, the job is a joy.

I also loved working on the Joslin De Lay Mysteries by Dennis Hamley. That series did an Ellis Peters type of thing – mysteries set in fourteenth-century Chaucerian times in England. Every time a new manuscript came in, it was just so exciting.

The other rewarding aspect of the job is getting letters from kids who have started reading as a result of one of your books. Being a commissioning editor for Scholastic is definitely the most fantastic job I've done.

Worst bit

When I started in the early nineties, Scholastic was a small company and a very energising place to work. As it grew it became more corporate and inevitably more political, which I didn't enjoy quite so much. Also, the hours were long. I used to start between 8:30 and 9 in the morning and arrive home at 7ish. And then I'd work on the train – so it was often a ten-hour day. Everyone in publishing works long hours. Publishing houses never have enough staff so people are always overworked.

Career path

I left Liverpool University in 1987 with an English degree. Someone suggested I do a course at the London College of Printing (LCP) at Elephant and Castle. The course gave me a diploma in Printing and Publishing Studies, and lasted four months. It gave me a great grounding in the basics of book production, and more importantly got me my first job in publishing.

I worked in the production department at Routledge (an academic publisher) for a year, before moving into the desk editing side. I always knew I wanted to be an editor, but don't regret my time spent in production, as it taught me the basics of how a book is put together and how much it costs. As a commissioning editor, you have to make decisions about spending money or not to produce the best book you can – an understanding and knowledge of the process is, in my view, a great asset.

After another year, an opportunity arose to work for a very creative and dynamic editor. I knew that I was unlikely to get promotion where I was (I am a great believer in making the most of your opportunities – no one else will do it for you!), so I leapt at the chance to gain more of an insight into the commissioning process. After a further nine months, I realised I had hit a brick wall, and also that I wasn't sufficiently interested in academic books to stay working in that field. I saw an advert for a desk editor at Scholastic and applied for it, children's books always being a passion of mine.

I was very fortunate, not only to get that job, but to have joined the company at a very exciting time, when it was expanding and there were a lot of opportunities for promotion. In the year I joined Point Horror was launched, and I was lucky enough to get asked to expand the Point list further, by setting up the Point Crime, Romance, Fantasy and SF lists. I stayed with the company for eight years, and only left after the birth of my second child. Sadly, I think the demands of working full time in the publishing industry don't fit very well with bringing up a family, so I am now freelancing and attempting to be a writer. I have two picture books coming out with Evans this year, and have written two adult and two children's novels.

Career Ladder

Commissioning editor at Scholastic
↑
Desk editor, Scholastic children's book publishers
↑
Editorial department, academic publishers
↑
Production assistant, academic publishers
↑
Diploma in Printing and Publishing Studies at London College of Printing
↑
English at university

TOP TIP

Look in trade journals for entry-level jobs. Try *The Bookseller*, *Publishing News* and *Printing World*.

REAL LIVES – THE ASSISTANT EDITOR, TROTMAN PUBLISHING

Bianca Knights, 27, originally from Ipswich, now in London

The job
Undertaking research for new and existing titles on behalf of the Commissioning Editor, and proofreading, copy-editing and proof collating for the Managing Editor.

Worst bit

As with most office jobs there is some administration involved, but I don't mind this as it makes a change – apart from the filing!

Best bit

Research for new titles and writing reports on submissions. I also enjoy the desk editorial work, i.e. the proofreading and copy-editing. Deciding on cover designs is fun. I also enjoy writing back cover copy.

Career path

I did a four-year French degree, and then taught English abroad for a year. By then I knew I wanted to work in book publishing and from there it was a long hard slog to get my first job as Editorial Assistant.

Career Ladder

Assistant editor at a publishing company
↑
Editorial assistant at a publishing company
↑
English language teacher, Réunion Island
↑
French at university

TOP TIP

Go to www.thebookseller.co.uk to find out more about publishing recruitment agencies.

REAL LIVES – THE PRODUCTION MANAGER, FABER AND FABER

Judith Young

The job

Managing the production team, schedules and suppliers, quality and cost control. Providing production support for the whole company and deputising for the Pre-Press and Production Director.

Worst bit
Trying to keep control of costs and tight schedules in a creative environment that needs to react quickly to external market pressures.

Best bit
Working in a very social and relaxed organisation with people who are passionate about the books they are working on and care deeply about the end result.

Career Ladder

Production Controller, then Production Manager, Faber and Faber
↑
Data Manager at a legal publisher
↑
Production Assistant, then Controller on loose leafs and digital products at legal publisher
↑
Master's degree in Publishing and Book Production at Stirling University

---

JARGON BUSTER

Pagemaker – a desktop publishing software programme used to lay out text and pictures.

REAL LIVES – THE HEAD OF PRODUCTION, SWEET AND MAXWELL LAW PUBLISHERS

Perry Coverley, 35

Best bit
I love working with books, managing people, managing a budget and being able to make my own decisions.

Worst bit
Managing people is also the worst bit about the job. It's

challenging and it can be difficult to get people to perform well all the time.

The job

I head up a team of 35 people. It's a management job. I'm responsible for departmental policy and the department's overall budget. I manage overhead expenditure and the people in the department. The department produces around 2,500 products a year – these include books, CDs and online products.

Career path

I did a print production course after university and that gave me some basic production skills. Through the course I got a job as a production assistant at Sweet and Maxwell. After a year I moved on to production controller and then I became a senior production controller and then a production manager and then head of production over about ten years.

The move from an assistant production controller up to a senior production controller is a case of being given more and more titles as your seniority increases. When I became a production manager the work became more managerial.

Career Ladder

Head of production
↑
Senior production controller
↑
Production controller
↑
Production assistant
↑
Print production course at the London College of Printing
↑
Politics and Economic Social History at university

> TOP TIP
>
> **All applications to jobs in publishing should be word perfect. Attention to detail is an essential part of most publishing jobs.**

Go to the Publishers Association website for loads of useful information on careers in publishing and vocational courses – www.publishers.org.uk.

Have a look at www.bookcareers.com for information on latest entry-level jobs and advice and information about a career in books.

WOMEN IN PUBLISHING
Women entering the industry should go to www.wipub.org.uk to find out what Women in Publishing is all about. A valuable organisation dedicated to information sharing, support and training, this site offers great advice and points out that although publishing is dominated by women, they still haven't broken the 'glass ceiling'. Indeed, a 2002 salary survey conducted by Bookcareers.com found that the average male salary was £26,123 compared to the female average salary of £21,644.

RELATED OCCUPATIONS

- Arts public relations
- Bookseller
- Indexing
- Lexicography
- Library services
- Newspapers and magazines
- Translating
- TV.

CHAPTER 8

New media

NEW MEDIA QUIZ

Here's a quick quiz to give you an idea of some of the skills needed to work in new media.

1) You're a web producer. You're in charge of setting up a new website. You've got to co-ordinate the designer, animator, coder, copywriter and a production team who are filming some video inserts to stream on the site.

   a) You're a fantastic strategic thinker. You draw up your master plan and give everyone deadlines. You're not frightened to hurry people along and keep all the suppliers on track.
   b) You're extremely creative, an ideas person, but you're a bit disorganised.
   c) You're a hard worker. You like to be a cog in a machine. Give you a task and you will complete it. But you don't want any overall responsibility.

2) You're a copywriter for the web. You have been asked to write the copy for a new health website for teenagers. You've been given some long-winded documents and asked to turn them into sparkling web copy.

a) You don't have the patience to trawl through pages and pages of writing.
b) You're interested in communicating clearly. It's worthwhile turning long complicated sentences into pithy writing for the web. That's what you love about the Internet – it makes communicating so quick, succinct and immediate.
c) You'd rather get someone else to do it.

3) **You've just landed a job as an assistant in a multi-media company. You're asked to research a new bit of software.**

a) You're not interested in new technology.
b) You can't believe you're being paid to research stuff you find so fascinating.
c) Soft what?

ANSWERS

1) The correct answer is (a). A web producer has to deal with clients and negotiate costs, and is responsible for delivering the site on time and according to the brief. This is a job for an extremely organised manager who is capable of overseeing a project but who is also diplomatic and good at getting the best out of people.

2) The correct answer is (b). Writing for the web, you will be either a journalist or copywriter. With most organisations requiring a web-based customer relationship, web writers work in a range of areas. In this instance you will probably need to be a specialist health writer. The key in writing for the web is being able to structure your copy to suit a site's format. It requires the ability to write succinctly and often the ability to load the page on to the system.

3) The correct answer is of course (b). Multi-media is an ever-changing environment driven by constantly emerging technology. It helps if you are fascinated by technological change. Who knows – you may be the next person to make a mint from thinking up a new way for us to receive information.

NEW MEDIA OVERVIEW

New media, multi-, interactive or digital media is an exciting area to work in. It's constantly changing and includes everything from the Internet and WAP phones to digital TV.

The digital revolution isn't coming – it's here already. The government wants to switch over UK television transmissions from analogue to digital signals by 2010. Already a significant proportion of the population have digital TVs. The digital revolution has increased the means and methods by which we can receive information and has shifted the viewers' place in the experience of receiving information. Now we can vote on issues on Five News, choose our favourite pop star and affect what happens on the screen. These days, viewers are part of the production team in that they create media output too.

Broadcasters are broadening their ideas about how to reach viewers. The new media division at the BBC includes BBC Online (Europe's largest website), Interactive Television and digital channels. It is thought Interactive TV will lead to the largest viewing changes since colour meant people could finally understand the snooker!

The next wave
No it's not a new film starring Bruce Willis – it's something you should know about if you want to work in new media. According to nextwave.org.uk, in the near future we're going to be able to get information everywhere, from our fridges to our cars.

'The "Next Wave", aka "ambient intelligence" or "pervasive", transparent" or "ubiquitous" computing will make up the domestic, consumer and business computing and communications environment of the future.

'The Next Wave Technologies will impact on all aspects of life: in the home, on the move, at work or out shopping. There will be a greater availability of "things that think" on behalf of the user, with a lowering of the knowledge threshold required to make constructive use of

> functionality, communications and processing. The trend
> has already started – "Internet" fridges, microwave ovens
> and other household and personal items are already
> appearing, but some believe they are currently of limited
> potential because the online services to support them are
> at an early stage of development. Provision of these
> services will follow soon enough, as will location-based
> services.'
>
> Source: www.nextwave.org.uk

New media now form a part of every sector from blue chip
companies to games developers, broadcasters and publishers.
New media include jobs for technical and creative people involved
in everything from programming to project management. Software
development and sales and marketing offer good entry-level
opportunities

Jobs in new media include:

- **Web designer** – works to a brief to create the look of the pages
  of an Internet site. Using programming techniques and Internet
  tools, the web designer works on the 'back end' systems to
  ensure the site works properly, and on the 'front end' to ensure
  it looks good and is easy to navigate. The web designer
  converts his or her ideas to the web via design software and
  code including HTML (hypertext mark-up language). Making
  changes in response to feedback from a client is an important
  part of a web designer's job.

- **Multi-media programmer** – writes the programmes that create
  multi-media products. These are designed to work on many
  'platforms' including interactive TV, CD-ROMs, DVDs, computer
  games and WAP phones. This is a technical and creative role.

- **Software engineer** (aka software developer or computer
  programmer) – designs software systems in response to a
  brief. The software engineer is responsible for maintaining and
  testing the software systems. Using programming applications
  and authoring tools, software engineers integrate text, video
  and sound. A software engineer may be supported by a coder.

CASH

Starting salaries are:

- **Web designer** – somewhere in the region of **£15,000**, going up to **£30,000** and above as career progresses.[6]

- **Multi-media programmer** – around **£15,000** to **£25,000**, going up to **£50,000** plus when established.[7]

- **Software engineer** – between **£18,000** and **£28,000**, increasing to a high of around **£60,000** when established.[7]

TOP TIP

Go to www.e-skills.com and www.prospects.ac.uk for more information on jobs and the IT industry.

REAL LIVES – THE WEB DESIGNER

Andrew Clarke, 25, South African born, now based in Newcastle

The job
I work freelance, which really suits me. At the moment I'm working on a new website aimed at teenagers. My brief is to come up with a cutting-edge look and feel. It's fun because I can go quite mad with the design.

Best bit
It's creative and satisfying when you see your final work go live. It's sociable. I'm always working with new teams of people on each job.

Worst bit
Clients don't always know what they want. So even when you have followed their brief they might want to change something fundamental to the design so you've got to basically start again.

[6] Figures from www.learndirect.co.uk
[7] Figures from Prospects website (www.prospects.ac.uk)

Also timings can be a problem. I'm always up against deadlines and I find deadlines a bit challenging! But I'm a perfectionist, so even if I do deliver a bit late the client is always really happy with the result.

TOP TIP

For some creative ideas read Creative Magazine at www.creativemag.com.

JARGON BUSTER

Java **– not coffee, but a programming language used on the Internet.**

REAL LIVES – THE NEW MEDIA EDITOR

Cait O'Riordan, Assistant Editor, BBC News On Demand

The job
I edit the output for broadband news and interactive television news. It's red-button stuff.

Best bit
I enjoy dealing with breaking news and I like the fact the job keeps changing as new ways of presenting news are developed in response to new technology.

Worst bit
That's got to be getting up at five in the morning on early starts or finishing late on late starts. The shifts are ten hours but I only work four days a week so that's a good thing.

Career Ladder

Assistant Editor, BBC News On Demand
↑
Senior Broadcast Journalist, BBC News On Demand
↑
Broadcast Journalist, BBC News On Demand
↑
Internet News Writer, ITN
↑
TV Documentary Producer
↑
National radio news
↑
Local radio news
↑
University degree

TOP TIP

Go to www.bbc.co.uk to find out more about interactive television news.

REAL LIVES – THE SENIOR WEB DEVELOPER

Leo Lapworth, 28, from London, works for Foxton's Estate Agents. Foxton's site has won the British Interactive Media Association's Grand Prix Award and Public Services Award.

How many visitors do you get?
Monthly we get over 4 million page impressions.

How many are there in your team?
Three.

How did you get your job?
I was head hunted from my CV on the net.

Best bit

I have never been bothered about the type of website I work on, it is the functionality and people that make it enjoyable. Foxton's aims to be the best London property website there is and I think the award proves we achieve that. The exciting thing is we are continuously trying to make it better. The web team also works on many of the internal systems at Foxton's, which allows us to meet different types of challenge. The web has been the most significant development for estate agents over the last few years and I see it continuing to make a big impact as we continue to explore other avenues such as SMS, email and any other avenues available.

Worst bit

There's never enough time to do everything you would like to, but I'd rather that than be bored!

Flexibility

The great thing about working in new media is that once you've got your skills you can work in most sectors.

JARGON BUSTER

Front end and *back end* – yes, it does sound weird. But it's really quite simple. The front end on an Internet site is what the user sees and the back end is the technical stuff that makes it happen.

REAL LIVES – THE MANAGING DIRECTOR OF A NEW MEDIA HEALTH CONSULTANCY

The job

I manage Health Technology Solutions Ltd, act as a consultant, account manager, project manager and – due to experience – occasional hands-on web development. Work focuses primarily on the health sector/NHS.

Worst bit

There isn't one!

Best bit
The satisfaction of providing solutions to client problems and
delivering solutions.

Career path
I began as an IT Support Officer in the NHS and progressed up
into IT Management. I took on the role of project
manager/director for national web-based project management
(initially by taking a chance and personally setting up a website
providing information on the NHS and being asked to join the
national team and do it for them instead). Then I left to join a
private sector company as an IT Director producing websites for
pharmaceutical companies in Health Promotion. After seeing the
company through floatation, I left to set up Health Technology
Solutions Ltd as an Internet/Web consultancy and development
supplier for health sector/NHS organisations and projects.

TOP TIP

**If gaming's your thing, go to the Independent Games
Developers' Trade Association – www.tiga.org.uk – to find
out more.**

RELATED OCCUPATIONS

● Applications developer

● Information technology consultant

● New business development

● Systems analyst

● Systems designer

● Technical author.

CHAPTER 9

Getting in and getting on

JOB HUNTING

Getting your first job in the media can be the most difficult part. First decide what it is you want to do by researching properly. Once you are focused on which area of the media you would like to work in, it will make it easier to land your perfect first job.

Look in the specialist press for advertised jobs (see below for details for each sector), check out the Internet and read Monday's *Guardian* for their weekly media jobs section. Also ask everyone and anyone you know who might be able to help you get some work experience. You will need to be resourceful. Don't be embarrassed to ask your parents' friends or your friend's parents' friends or your parents' parents' friends! Leave no stone unturned. They will understand – everybody had to start somewhere! Go to www.work-experience.org for more information on work experience.

TRAINING

Even if you are a graduate, vocational training may be useful to give you the edge over other candidates (see below for contact details for each sector). It's a good idea to do some work experience first so that you can decide whether you will enjoy working in your chosen area. If you can't afford to pay for training, don't despair. In a lot of media jobs you can learn on the job. You just need to be able to throw yourself in at the deep end.

INTERNSHIP AND GRADUATE TRAINEESHIPS

Some of the larger broadcasters, newspapers and publishing houses offer limited places on their graduate trainee programmes. These offer excellent training and possibilities for career advancement. While doing your research, find out what large organisations like the BBC and Penguin can offer you. It is difficult to get on to a training scheme, but most organisations provide a detailed description of what they are looking for on their websites. Find out about these are early as possible so that you can apply in time and also fill in any gaps that you may need to.

NETWORKING

Getting your foot in the door and then progressing up the media career ladder will depend on your networking skills. Because so many media jobs require long hours in stressful conditions, being a 'people person' is an important part of many jobs. If you make friends on every job you work on, you will have a network of colleagues to tell you about new job opportunities. Word of mouth is a powerful tool in the media. We've done some networking for you! Scouring the country to find those in the know, we've asked for advice from them so you can get ahead and get on. Read on for their gems of wisdom!

YOUR CV

People who break into media are more likely to do so by sending in a CV and covering letter to a specific person in an organisation than by answering a job advertisement. Skillset did a survey of freelancers working in the audio-visual industries and discovered that between one-fifth and a half of those starting out got their first job by contacting their employer rather than answering an ad.

However, a lot of CVs just go 'on file' – put in a drawer somewhere never to see the light of day again. It will help if you target where you are sending your CV.

● Think about where you are sending your CV. Research companies with products you love. If you love a particular book, find out who published it; if you love a television programme, find out who made it.

● Do some research in the specialist press to find out what is being made now. (See details below.) Inside knowledge goes a long way. It makes you look professional and focused and you can match your skills to a particular project.

It also helps if your CV looks good and is word perfect. CHECK AND DOUBLE-CHECK YOUR CV FOR MISTAKES. Finding mistakes in a CV drives employers mad and makes you look sloppy. Most entry-level jobs will require administration in some form, for which attention to detail will be important. Spelling mistakes give the impression that you are not good at detail and that possibly you haven't put much effort in.

Find out the name of the correct person to send your CV to. Otherwise you will look lazy. And spell it right. Ever got junk mail through the post that spells your name wrong or gets your gender wrong? Well that's the kind of impression you want to avoid.

TOP TIP

Skillsformedia at www.skillsformedia.com can help you create the perfect CV, as can Channel 4's IDEASFACTORY at www.ideasfactory.com.

INTERVIEW TIPS

Most of how to behave in an interview is common sense and you've probably been through it before – but just to refresh your memory:

- Never go unprepared to an interview. Always research the output of any company you are going to see. If you turn up at a publisher and don't know what books they publish, they will think you aren't interested. If you manage to secure an interview with a TV company and haven't watched any of their programmes they'll wonder why you turned up! Don't blow precious chances – do your research before the interview.

- People in the media are passionate about what they do. You will need to convince them that you are passionate about their area too. Have a few ideas up your sleeve in case you can impress an interviewer with your creativity. Remember, in many sectors the 16–34 market is key because advertisers chase that age group. There's big money in TV series that have high ratings in that age group, for example. As a younger person your ideas will be taken seriously. Go to **IDEAS**FACTORY (www.ideasfactory.com) for some inspiration.

- Shake hands with the interviewer when you walk into the room. Stand up straight. And when you leave, shake hands again and thank them for their time.

- Smile, and try to convey what the interview is – a fantastic opportunity for you to break into the industry of your dreams.

- Carefully choose what to wear. Inside information helps, so ask someone who works in the industry if you can. You don't always need to wear a suit but you do always need to wear clean clothes!

- Keep your hands in your lap if you're feeling nervous. You will look less nervous if your hands are still.

- Look people straight in the eye.

- It's not essential, but a letter written to the interviewer to say how much you enjoyed meeting him or her comes across as courteous.

TV AND FILM

Here's some advice from those who know on routes into the industry:

'Exhaust any contacts you might have, ask everyone if they know anyone who works in TV. Unfortunately I didn't know anyone, but I got my runner's job from an ad in the *Guardian* – it was luck. Blag it the whole way too! I started filming on a shoot and I'd never done it before. Be confident, but also be a little bit humble and nice to people. It's about skill and vision and creativity but ultimately it's about people. There are always 20 other people who could do your job.'

Freelance Kids' TV director

'If you want to become a broadcast journalist, do one of the specific broadcast journalism courses. I did mine after I graduated with a degree in French. The best piece of advice I ever got was to start out in independent local radio. They've got so much less money than somewhere like the BBC so you are very quickly given a lot of responsibility as it's all hands on deck. You will be paid appallingly but it will stand you in good stead for the future. It's incredibly hard work and probably will include night-time shifts, but you've just got to bite the bullet for about a year and a half. You'll learn more than you imagined possible.'

TV News Reporter

'I got my running job through a friend. I put the word out that I was looking for a running job. He's now moved on to a job as an editing assistant. To be a runner you've just got to keep focused on what you want out of it. You certainly don't need brains to do running, just staying power!'

Post-production runner for TV and video

'When I was working as a production assistant on the *Today* programme John Humphrys gave me the best piece of advice of my career. He told me to go to local radio and get my experience there. He was right – you get amazing experience and you can make mistakes and learn from them in front of a smaller audience.'

TV News presenter

Becoming a presenter

To become a TV presenter you need to make a **showreel**. There's some really useful information about how to put one together on the Channel 4 website: www.channel4.com/careers.

They say you need to:

- Grab the viewer's attention in the first minute.

- Make it fun and interesting.

- Keep it short – four to five minutes.

- Include a mix of short scenes (perhaps a live outside report and a mock interview).

- Do it on the cheap – ask family and friends.

- When sending out your showreel always send a copy, not your original – you've unlikely to get it back!

'Without a doubt television is one of the most fun jobs you can have. But if you want financial security you should go into the management side of the business.'

'As programmes are made with smaller and smaller budgets, these days technical skills are becoming increasingly important. Being able to work a camera, do the sound and editing are all useful skills nowadays, even for a producer. To become a producer, I would advise that you try and get a running or administrative job with a big company like Granada or the BBC and be trained in-house. Independents have to throw you out once your contract is up because they can't afford to keep you on. Everyone's salary has to come out of a programme budget. If you do want to work for an independent, try a larger company that has a high turnover of popular programmes and is likely to have more money to be able to keep you on for a bit. It's easy to work out which the successful companies are. Just watch TV! The name of the production company that made a programme will always be displayed in the credits at the end. Most production companies have their own websites with contact details.'

Freelance TV Producer

'Do what I did and start out getting some work experience. When you do land a job as a production assistant, don't expect to be making films immediately! Although a production assistant's job can be exciting, it's a secretarial role - very few boys do it because of that. But in the end most producers are men.'

Film Production Assistant

'Write to a casting director and volunteer to work for free. It's good to get DV skills as you are likely to have to film auditions.'

Film Assistant Casting Director

'Join the BBC. You get good training and lots of money. Phone around all the production companies to start you on your career path. Either get a runner's position or find an assistant/secretarial role in a development team.'

Script Editor

SPECIALIST PRESS

Broadcast (www.broadcastnow.co.uk)
Ariel (in-house BBC magazine – call 01709 364 721)
AV – Audio Visual Magazine (www.avmag.co.uk)
Screen International (www.screendaily.com)
Campaign (www.brandrepublic.com)
Media Week (www.mediaweek.co.uk)
Press Gazette (www.pressgazette.co.uk)
The Stage (www.thestage.co.uk)
Televisual

WEBSITES

www.4rfv.co.uk
www.bbc.co.uk

www.filmcast.org
www.film-tv.co.uk
www.guardian.co.uk
www.ideasfactory.com
www.jobsintv.com
www.productionbase.co.uk
www.shootingpeople.org
www.startintv.com
www.ukscreen.com

COURSE INFORMATION
British Film Institute (www.bfi.org.uk/education/courses)
Learn Direct (www.learndirect.co.uk). Tel: 0800 100 900
Skills for Media (www.skillsformedia.com).

RADIO

Some words of advice:

'You do need to be the right kind of person to present. You've got to be talkative and able to interact with your listeners. If you are the right kind of personality, then it's possible to make it. You need to have passion because you have to be able to get up the same energy time and again and you've got to put yourself a bit out there. Community radio is a great place to start. While you're working you can get a demo together – it will help you make your next career move.'

Community Radio DJ

'A postgraduate broadcasting course with an emphasis on practical skills is useful. Work experience is essential. I started a magazine at university and that helped me get on the course and my first job.'

Researcher on radio documentaries

SPECIALIST PRESS
Broadcast magazine
Ariel (the magazine for BBC staff)
Media Guardian on Mondays

WEBSITES
www.bbc.co.uk
www.guardian.co.uk
www.ideasfactory.com
www.hospitalradio.co.uk
www.mediauk.com
www.radiosupport.co.uk
www.radio-now.co.uk
www.ukradio.com

COURSE INFORMATION
Broadcast Journalism Training Council
Tel: 01778 440 025. Email: secretary@btjc.org.uk
Website: www.bjtc.org.uk

Commercial Radio Companies Association
Tel: 020 7306 2603. Email: info@crca.co.uk

Radio Academy
Email: info@radioacademy.org
Website: www.radioacademy.org/masterclass

NEWSPAPERS AND MAGAZINES

Some tips on getting on in newspapers and magazines.

'I would say definitely do a journalism course. I did one after university. I'm glad I chose this route as my degree in politics and sociology was fascinating and I learnt excellent writing and researching skills whilst doing my degree. These are useful skills for news reporting. What I regret is not doing more research before I chose my postgraduate journalism course. Some courses prepare you more for national newspapers and have links with those and others prepare you more for local newspapers. I didn't realise this when I found my course. Always ask what aspect of journalism your course is geared towards, then you can go in with your eyes open. Also, find out where ex-graduates have got placements. For example, I know people often get good placements after the Cardiff course – Cardiff School of Journalism, Media and Cultural Studies, www.cf.ac.uk/jomec/ – as it's considered one of the best places to do a postgrad journalism course. After all, it's likely you will have to pay for the course yourself, so make sure you get value for money and ensure whatever course you choose is approved by the National Council for the Training of Journalists (NCTJ), www.nctj.com/.'

Senior Reporter, local newspaper

'Do work experience in a magazine or newspaper office. The key is to try to make yourself noticed without being obnoxious. Most bottom-rung jobs in magazines don't require a huge amount of talent: you're most likely to be taken on if you come across as likeable, smiley and efficient. These days, people spend a vast amount of their lives at work, so when they take on junior staff, they are looking for people who'll be nice to have around and who'll get the job done with minimum fuss.'

Magazine Editor

'There isn't a traditional career path for a picture editor. Interest in photography and images is essential and a lot of picture editors come from a photographic background. You don't have to be particularly academic. I've got a degree but it's not in any way a necessity for the job. If you want to work for a newspaper, choose carefully, as some papers place a lot more emphasis on images than others. For example, in my opinion, the *Guardian* or the *Independent* use more exciting images than most other national papers. Make sure you look at how different papers use images and try to work for the one that appeals to you most. Getting work experience on a picture desk is a good way to find out if the job is for you. You will be taken more seriously if you can display a real interest and love of pictures and photography. Securing a work experience position isn't easy. Try using any contact you can – ask everyone you know in case they know anyone who works on a local paper, magazine or even a national. Failing that, be really persistent. You might just catch someone on the right day.'

Picture Editor, national newspaper

'I didn't do a journalism course. But a lot of journalists find them useful. I think the key is to start writing as early as possible. Find opportunities to write at school and university. Start freelancing as soon as you can, send off ideas to editors and make as many contacts as possible. A local newspaper is an excellent place to start after university.'

International News Agency Reporter

SPECIALIST PRESS

Guardian Media Section (www.mediaguardian.co.uk)
Press Gazette (www.pressgazette.co.uk)
Ariel (in-house BBC magazine – call 01709 364 721)

WEBSITES

BBC (www.bbc.co.uk)
National Union of Journalists (www.nuj.com)

COURSE INFORMATION

Broadcast Journalism Training Council
Tel: 01778 440025 Email: secretary@btjc.org.uk
Website: www.bjtc.org.uk

National Council for the Training of Journalists (NCTJ)
Latton Bush Centre, Southern Way, Harlow, Essex CM18 7BL
Tel: 01279 430009. Website: www.nctj.com

Newspaper Society
Bloomsbury House, Bloomsbury Square, 74–77 Great Russell
Street, London WC1B 3DA. Tel: 020 7636 7014.
Website: www.newspapersoc.org.uk

BOOKS AND PUBLISHING

Some words of wisdom:

'Do get some design and production training. For example, to become a book designer you will need to be trained in typography and layout. Once trained, look for job advertisements in the specialised press or approach a publishing recruitment agency to see if they can find you an entry-level position like a production assistant. Other routes in include work experience.'

Assistant Editor, book publishing

'I'd advise doing a relevant postgraduate course that creates some sort of basic understanding of the industry and then join a publishing recruitment agency. Work experience is useful if you've got nothing else happening. In my experience, however, publishers tend to have a lot of people doing work experience at any one time with little hope of a job at the end. You are more likely to secure a position through the course/recruitment agency route.'

Head of Production, book publishing

'For specialist roles in production and design some relevant qualification is very helpful, but getting work experience and temporary work in trade publishing shows enthusiasm and commitment.'

Production Manager, book publishing

'You've got to make your own career in publishing. You need to be really keen and make your own opportunities. I'll never forget a friend of mine who started at Routledge at the same time as me. She went to every department asking them what they did and finding out what the opportunities were for her. You have to be as enthusiastic and self-motivated as that to get on.

'Other routes to get into publishing include the traditional secretarial route, though I would advise going for editorial/marketing/production assistant-type jobs if you don't want to get sidelined into becoming a PA. Working in bookselling will also give you a fabulously commercial insight into what sells, and what stays resolutely on the shelves, and I can recommend that as another route in – though be warned, this is more likely to get you into the marketing side, than the editorial side.

'I would also suggest that if you are at college, get a job selling books in your holidays, do some temping for a publishing company or anything at all connected with publishing, which shows you are willing and able. I would also recommend that you do as my friend did, and try and understand all the processes involved in publishing a book – when it works it is a cohesive process, which demands good communication and understanding of your colleagues' problems. If you can do that, then you will go far!'

Commissioning Editor, book publishing

SPECIALIST PRESS
The Bookseller (www.thebookseller.com)
Printing World
Publishing News (www.publishingnews.co.uk)

ORGANISATIONS AND WEBSITES
Association of On-Line Publishers (AOP)
Queens House, 28 Kingsway, London WC2B 6JR
Website: www.ukaop.org.uk

Book Careers (www.bookcareers.com)

Booksellers' Association of the United Kingdom and Ireland Ltd (BA)
Minster House, 272 Vauxhall Bridge Road, London SW1V 1BA
Tel: 020 7834 5477. Website: www.booksellers.org.uk

Periodicals Training Council (PTC)
Queen's House, 28 Kingsway, London WC2B 6JR
Tel: 020 7404 4166. Website: www.ppa.co.uk/ptc

Publishers Association (PA)
29b Montague Street, London WC1B 5BW
Tel: 020 7691 9191. Website: www.publishers.org.uk

COURSES
Publishers Association (www.publishers.org.uk)

Publishing National Training Organisation
55/56 Lincolns Inn Fields, London WC2A 3LJ
Website: www.publishingnto.co.uk

Go to www.thebookseller.co.uk to find out more about publishing
recruitment agencies.

NEW MEDIA

Advice from people working in new media:

'I come from an art background and I taught myself
all the back end stuff. I would say do a course if you
want to, but the key is to start designing. Do
websites for your friends and let people know what
you're doing. If you're good, word will soon get
around. But market yourself too. Once you've done a
few sites, get business cards, set up your own
website and start pitching for business.'

Web Designer

'Work in local papers or local radio or in online news
for local TV. Do at least two years in local news. For
a job at BBC Online that news experience will give
you a good head start.'

Assistant Editor, BBC News On Demand

SPECIALIST PRESS
Creation magazine (www.creationmag.co.uk)
Creative Review (www.creativereview.co.uk)
New Media Age (www.nma.com)
Revolution magazine (www.uk.revolutionmagazine.com)

ORGANISATIONS AND WEBSITES
British Computer Society (BCS)
1 Sanford Street
Swindon
Wiltshire SN1 1HJ
Tel: 01793 417 424
Website: www.bcs.org.uk

British Interactive Multimedia Association (BIMA)
Briarlea House
Southend Road
South Green
Billericay
Essex CM11 2PR
Tel: 01277 658107
Website: www.bima.co.uk

British Web Design and Marketing Association (BWDMA)
PO Box 3227
London NW9 9LX
Tel: 020 8204 2474
Website: www.bwdma.co.uk/

Institution of Analysts and Programmers (IAP)
Charles House
36 Culmington Road
London W13 9NH
Tel: 020 8567 2118
Website: www.iap.org.uk

Institute for the Management of Information Systems (IMIS)
5 Kingfisher House
New Mill Road
Orpington
Kent BR5 3QG

Tel: 0700 00 23456
Website: www.imis.org.uk

COURSE INFORMATION
British Film Institute (BFI)
21 Stephen Street
London W1P 1PL
Tel: 020 7255 1444
Website: www.bfi.org.uk

Independent Games Developers' Trade Association
(www.tiga.org.uk)

Skillset (Sector Skills Council for the Audio Visual Industries)
Prospect House
80–110 New Oxford Street
London WC1A 1HB
Tel: 020 7520 5757
Website: www.skillset.org

CHAPTER 10

The information

If you're interested in any of the careers in this book, now's the time to start researching further. If you can't find the right information, ask. With loads of interactive services available like LearnDirect it is always possible to email a specialist for some specific careers advice. Go to www.learndirect.co.uk for more information.

GENERAL

Benn's Media Directory, CMP Data and Information Services, annual (February)
Careers in Journalism, Kogan Page (8th edn)
Guardian, Guardian Newspapers Ltd (www.guardian.co.uk), daily
Guardian Media Guide, Atlantic Books, annual
Press Gazette, Quantum Publishing, weekly
Willings Press Guide, Hollis Publishing Ltd, annual

TV AND FILM

BKSTS – The Moving Image Society
Pinewood Studios, Pinewood Road
Iver Heath
Buckinghamshire SLO ONH
Tel: 01753 656656
Website: www.bksts.com

British Academy of Film and Television Arts (BAFTA)
195 Piccadilly
London W1J 9LN
Tel: 020 7734 0022
Website: www.bafta.org

Office of Communications (OFCOM)
Riverside House
Southwark
London SE1 9HA
Tel: 020 7981 3040
Website: www.ofcom.org.uk

Producers' Alliance for Cinema and Television (PACT)
45 Mortimer Street
London W1W 8HJ
Tel: 020 7331 6000
Website: www.pact.co.uk

Royal Television Society
Holborn Hall
100 Gray's Inn Road
London WC1X 8AL
Tel: 020 7430 1000
Website: www.rts.org.uk

Skillset and Skillsformedia
Prospect House
80–110 New Oxford Street
London WC1A 1HB
Tel: 020 7520 5757
Websites: www.skillset.org and www.skillsformedia.com

UNIONS, GUILDS AND TRADE ASSOCIATIONS

Advertising Producers' Association
26 Noel Street
London W1F 8GT
Tel: 020 7434 2651
Website: www.a-p-a.net

Amalgamated Engineering and Electrical Union (AMICUS)
Hayes Court
West Common Road
Hayes, Bromley
Kent BR2 7AU
Tel: 020 8462 7755
Website: www.aeeu.org.uk

Broadcasting, Entertainment, Cinematograph and Theatre Union
(BECTU)
373–377 Clapham Road
London SW9 9BT
Tel: 020 7346 0900
Website: www.bectu.org.uk

Broadcast Journalism Training Council
18 Miller's Close
Rippingale, near Bourne
Lincolnshire PE10 OTH
Tel: 01778 440 025
Website: www.bjtc.org.uk

Casting Directors' Guild
PO Box 34403
London W6 OYG
Tel: 020 8741 1951
Website: www.castingdirectorsguild.co.uk

Directors' Guild of Great Britain
Acorn House
314–320 Gray's Inn Road
London WC1X 8DP
Tel: 020 7248 4343
Website: www.dggb.co.uk

Guild of British Camera Technicians
GBCT, c/o Panavision UK
Metropolitan Centre
Bristol Road
Greenford
Middlesex UB6 8GD
Tel: 020 8813 1999
Website: www.gbct.org

Guild of Location Managers
20 Euston Centre
Regent's Place
London NW1 3JH
Tel: 020 7387 8787
Website: www.golm.org.uk

Guild of TV Cameramen
April Cottage
The Chalks
Chew Magna
Bristol BS40 8SN
Website: www.gtc.org.uk

Guild of Vision Mixers
Website: www.guildofvisionmixers.co.uk

Institute of Broadcast Sound
27 Old Gloucester Street
London WC1N 3XX
Website: www.ibs.org.uk

Music Video Producers Association
26 Noel Street
London W1F 8GY
Tel: 020 7434 2651
Website: www.mvpa.co.uk

National Union of Journalists (NUJ)
Headland House
308 Gray's Inn Road
London WC1X 8DP
Tel: 020 7278 7916
Website: www.nuj.org.uk

Production Guild of Great Britain
Pinewood Studios
Pinewood Road
Iver Heath
Buckinghamshire SLO ONH
Tel: 01753 651 767
Website: www.productionguild.com

Production Managers' Association
Ealing Studios
Ealing Green
London W5 5EP
Tel: 020 8758 8699
Website: www.pma.org.uk

Professional Lighting and Sound Association
38 St Leonards Road
Eastbourne BN21 3UT
Tel: 01323 410335
Website: www.plasa.org

Society of Television Lighting Directors
Website: www.stld.org.uk

Teledwyr Annibynnool Cymru (TAC)
Website: www.teledwyr.com

Women in Film and Television
6 Langley Street
London WC2H 9JA
Tel: 020 7240 4875
Website: www.wftv.org.uk

Writers' Guild of Great Britain
15 Britannia Street
London WC1X 9JN
Tel: 020 7833 0777
Website: www.writersguild.org.uk

RADIO

Broadcast Journalism Training Council
(see information under Film and TV, above)

Commercial Radio Companies Association
Tel: 020 7306 2603
Website: www.crca.co.uk/workinginradio.htm

Community Media Association
Tel: 0114 279 5219
Website: www.commedia.org.uk/accessradio/index.htm

NEWSPAPER AND MAGAZINES

Daily Mail and General Trust plc
Head and Registered Office
Northcliffe House
2 Derry Street
London W8 5TT
Tel: 020 7938 6629
Website: www.dmgt.co.uk

EMAP
40 Bernard Street
London WC1N 1LW
Tel: 020 7278 1452
Website: www.emap.com

Guardian Media Group plc
75 Farringdon Road
London EC1M 3JY
Tel: 020 7278 2332
Website: www.gmgplc.co.uk

Haymarket Publishing Ltd
174 Hammersmith Road
London W6 7JP
Tel: 020 8267 5000
Website: www.haymarketgroup.co.uk/

IPC Magazines
King's Reach Tower
Stamford Street
London SE1 9LS
Tel: 020 7261 5000
Website: www.ipc.co.uk/

National Council for the Training of Journalists (NCTJ)
Latton Bush Centre
Southern Way
Harlow
Essex CM18 7BL
Tel: 01279 430009
Website: www.nctj.com

National Union of Journalists (NUJ)
Acorn House
308 Gray's Inn Road
London WC1X 8DP
Tel: 020 7278 7916
Website: www.nuj.org.uk

Newspaper Society
Bloomsbury House
Bloomsbury Square
74–77 Great Russell Street
London WC1B 3DA
Tel: 020 7636 7014
Website: www.newspapersoc.org.uk

Newsquest
Unecol House
819 London Road
North Cheam
Surrey SM3 9BN
Tel: 020 8329 9244
Website: www.newsquest.co.uk

Periodical Publishers Association Ltd (PPA)
Queens House
28 Kingsway
London WC2B 6JR
Tel: 020 7404 4166
Website: www.ppa.co.uk

Press Association
292 Vauxhall Bridge Road
London SW1V 1AE
Tel: 020 7963 7000
Website: www.pa.press.net/

Trinity Mirror plc
One Canada Square
Canary Wharf
London E14 5AP
Tel: 020 7293 3000
Website: www.trinitymirror.com

NEW MEDIA

British Computer Society
www.bcs.org.uk

British Interactive Multimedia Association
www.bima.co.uk

British Web Design and Marketing Association
www.bwdma.co.uk

e-skills UK
www.e-skills.com

Independent Games Developers Trade Association
www.tiga.org.uk

Institute of Analysts and Programmers
www.iap-online.org.uk

International Games Developers Association
www.igda.org

National Computing Centre (NCC)
www.ncc.co.uk

PUBLISHING

Association of Learned and Professional Society Publishers
South House
The Street
Clapham
Worthing
West Sussex BN13 3UU
Tel: 01903 871 686
Website: www.alpsp.org.uk

Association of On-Line Publishers (AOP)
Queens House
28 Kingsway
London WC2B 6JR
Website: www.ukaop.org.uk

Booksellers Association of The United Kingdom and Ireland Ltd
(BA)
Minster House
272 Vauxhall Bridge Road
London SW1V 1BA
Tel: 020 7834 5477
Website: www.booksellers.org.uk

Cambridge University Press
The Edinburgh Building
Shaftesbury Road
Cambridge CB2 2RU
Tel: 01223 325757
Website: www.cup.cam.ac.uk/

Chrysalis Group plc
The Chrysalis Building
Bramley Road
London W10 6SP
Tel: 020 7221 2213
Website: www.chrysalis.com

Financial Times Group
1 Southwark Bridge
London SE1 9HL
Website: www.news.ft.com/home/uk/

Haymarket Publishing Ltd
174 Hammersmith Road
London W6 7JP
Tel: 020 8267 5000
Website: www.haymarketgroup.co.uk/
IPC Magazines
King's Reach Tower
Stamford Street
London SE1 9LS
Tel: 020 7261 5000
Website: www.ipc.co.uk/

The Irish Book Publishers Association
43–44 Temple Bar
Dublin 2
Tel: +00 353 (0)1 670 7393
Website: www.publishingireland.com/

Macmillan Publishers Ltd
4 Crinan Street
London N1 9XW
Tel: 020 7843 3600
Website: www.macmillan.co.uk

Music Publishers Association Ltd
3rd Floor
Strandgate
18–20 York Buildings
London WC2N 6JU
Tel: 020 7839 7779

News International
News International Syndication
PO Box 481
London E1 9BD
Tel: 020 7782 5400
Website: www.syndication.newsint.co.uk

Oxford University Press (OUP)
Great Clarendon Street
Oxford OX2 6DP
Tel: 01865 556 767
Website: www.oup.co.uk

Pearson
80 Strand
London WC2R 0RL
Tel: 020 7010 2000
Website: www.pearson.com

Pearson Education
Edinburgh Gate
Harlow
Essex CM20 2JE
Tel: 01279 623928
Website: www.pearsoneduc.com/

Penguin Books Ltd
Bath Road
Harmondsworth
West Drayton
Middlesex UB7 0DA

Periodical Publishers Association Ltd (PPA)
Queens House
28 Kingsway
London WC2B 6JR
Tel: 020 7404 4166
Website: www.ppa.co.uk

Periodicals Training Council (PTC)
Contact details as above
Website: www.ppa.co.uk/ptc

Publishers Association (PA)
29b Montague Street
London WC1B 5BW
Tel: 020 7691 9191
Website: www.publishers.org.uk

Publishing National Training Organisation
55/56 Lincolns Inn Fields
London WC2A 3LJ
Website: www.publishingnto.co.uk

Publishing Training Centre
45 East Hill
Wandsworth
London SW18 2QZ
Tel: 020 8874 2718
Website: www.train4publishing.co.uk

Reed Business Information
Quadrant House
The Quadrant
Sutton
Surrey SM2 5AS
Tel: 020 8652 3500
Website: www.reedbusiness.co.uk

Reed Elsevier
25 Victoria Street
London SW1H 0EX
Tel: 020 7930 7077
Website: www.reed-elsevier.com

Scottish Publishers Association
Scottish Book Centre
137 Dundee Street
Edinburgh EH11 1BG
Tel: 0131 228 6866
Website: www.scottishbooks.org

Society for Editors and Proofreaders (SfEP)
Riverbank House
1 Putney Bridge Approach
London SW6 3JD
Tel: 020 7736 3278
Website: www.sfep.org.uk

Society of Picture Researchers and Editors
455 Finchley Road
London NW3 6HN

Society of Young Publishers
Endeavour House
189 Shaftesbury Avenue
London WC2H 3TJ
Website: www.thesyp.org.uk

Trinity Mirror plc
One Canada Square
Canary Wharf
London E14 5AP
Tel: 020 7293 3000
Website: www.trinitymirror.com